小马外语

扫 描 二 维 码
收听全书音频

中英对照彩绘珍藏版

夜莺与玫瑰

王尔德作品集

（英）奥斯卡·王尔德（Oscar Wilde） 著

林徽因 译

张叔筠 绘

化学工业出版社

·北京·

关于作者奥斯卡·王尔德

奥斯卡·王尔德(Oscar Wilde，1854~1900年)，英国著名作家、戏剧家、诗人。19世纪80年代美学运动的主力，90年代颓废派运动的先驱。其作品辞藻华美、立意新颖、观点鲜明。

童年与少年时代

1854年，王尔德生于爱尔兰都柏林，父亲是外科医生，母亲是诗人。

1864年，王尔德就读位于恩尼斯基伦的波托拉皇家学校，他钟情于自然美景和希腊文学。在校最后一年获得代表古典文学成绩最佳荣誉的波托拉金质奖章。

1871年，年仅17岁的王尔德获得都柏林三一学院奖学金。

1874年，王尔德进入牛津大学莫德林学院学习。

1878年，王尔德在牛津大学就读的最后一年，他不但学习成绩名列前茅，而且诗作获奖，得奖的诗作由学校出资付梓，成为王尔德第一本出版的作品。

王尔德在牛津大学受到了沃尔特·佩特及约翰·拉斯金的审美观念影响，并接触了新黑格尔派哲学、达尔文进化论和拉斐尔前派的作品，这为他之后成为唯美主义先锋作家确立了方向。

意气风发那些年

1880 年，谈吐机智、特立独行的王尔德在伦敦社交界已经小有名气。

1882 年，王尔德在美国进行了一次精彩的巡回讲座。

两年后他与康斯坦斯·劳埃德恋爱成婚，两个儿子西里尔与维维安亦分别在 1885 年与 1886 年出生。

1887 年，王尔德成为《妇女世界》杂志的执行总编辑，期间他发表了一些小说、评论和诗。

1888 年，出版《快乐王子故事集》。

1890 年，在报纸上连载长篇小说《道林·格雷的画像》奠定颓废艺术家的地位。

小说创作之后他又发表了散文，都十分成功，但真正为王尔德赢得名誉的是他的戏剧作品。如《温德米尔夫人的扇子》

《理想的丈夫》等，都是一时绝唱。可以说他的每一部戏剧作品都受到热烈欢迎。

王尔德的童话王国

王尔德的童话被誉为"世界上最美的童话"。他的早期作品中有两本童话集：《快乐王子故事集》和《石榴之家》已载入英国儿童文学史册。在王尔德优美细腻的文笔下，是他的一颗纯美纯善、难以泯灭的童心。王尔德的童话，语言纯正优美堪称典范，意境高洁益人心智，每一个孩子和每一个不想长大的大人都应该来读一读。

其中广为人知的童话有《夜莺与玫瑰》《快乐王子》《忠实的朋友》《了不起的火箭》《星星男孩》《少年国王》《自私的巨人》等等。这些童话故事语言华丽唯美，情节纯真生动，堪称完美世界的化身。愿你细细品读，从中体会人间的冷暖，领悟人生的哲理。

译者的话

2017 年 1 月

目录 CONTENTS

夜莺与玫瑰

"她说我若为她采得一朵红玫瑰，便与我跳舞。"青年学生哭着说，"但我全园里何曾有一朵红玫瑰？"

夜莺在橡树上的巢中听见，从叶丛里向外看，心中诧异。

青年学生哭道："我园中并没有红玫瑰！"他秀眼里满含着泪珠。"哎！幸福竟靠着这些小东西！古圣贤书我已读完，哲学的玄秘我已彻悟，然而因为求一朵红玫瑰不得，我的生活便这样难堪。"

夜莺叹道："真情人竟在这里。以前我虽不曾认识，我却夜夜歌唱他：我夜夜将他的一桩桩事告诉星辰，如今我见着他了。他的头发黑如风信子花，嘴唇红比他所切盼的玫瑰，但是挚情已使他脸色憔悴，烦恼已在他眉端印下痕迹。"

青年学生又低声自语："王子会在明晚的宴会上跳舞，我的爱人也将与会。我若为她采得红玫瑰，她就和我跳舞直到天明，我若为她采得红玫瑰，我将把她抱在怀里。她的头，在我肩上枕着，她的手，在我手中握着。但我园里没有红玫瑰，我只能寂寞地坐着，看她从我跟前走过。她不理睬我，我的心将要粉碎了。"

"这真是个真情人。"夜莺又说，"我所歌唱的，是他尝受的苦楚：在我是乐的，在他却是悲痛。爱果然是件非常的东西。比翡翠还珍重，比玛瑙更宝贵。珍珠、榴石买不到它，黄金亦不能作它的代价，因为它不是在市场上出售的，也不是商人贩卖的东西。"

青年学生说："乐师们将在舞会上弹弄丝竹，我那爱人也将随着弦琴的音节舞蹈。她舞得那么翩翩，莲步都不着地，华服的少年们就会艳羡地围着她。但她不同我跳舞，因我没有为她采到红玫瑰。"于是他扑倒在草里，两手掩着脸哭泣。

绿色的小壁虎说："他为什么哭泣？"说完就竖起尾巴从他跟前跑过。

蝴蝶正追着阳光飞舞，也问道："唉，怎么了？"

金盏花亦向她的邻居低声探问："唉，怎么了？"

夜莺说："他为着一朵红玫瑰哭泣。"

他们叫道："为了一朵红玫瑰！真是笑话！"那小壁

虎本来就刻薄，更是大笑。

然而夜莺了解那青年学生烦恼里的秘密，她静坐在橡树枝上细想"爱"的玄妙。

忽然她张起棕色的双翼，冲天飞去。她穿过那如同影子一般的树林，如同影子一般地，她飞出了花园。

草地当中站着一株艳美的玫瑰树，夜莺看见那树，向前飞去落在一根小小的枝头上。

她叫道："给我一朵红玫瑰，我为你唱我最婉转的歌。"

可是那树摇头。

"我的玫瑰是白的，"那树回答她，"白如海涛的泡沫，白过山巅上的积雪。请你到古日晷旁找我兄弟，或许他能应你所求。"

于是夜莺飞到日晷旁边那丛玫瑰上。

她又叫道："给我一朵红玫瑰，我为你唱最醉人的歌。"

可是那树摇头。

"我的玫瑰是黄的，"那树回答她，"黄如琥珀座上美人鱼的头发，黄过草地上未被割除的金水仙。请你到那边青年学生窗下找我兄弟，或许他能应你所求。"

于是夜莺飞到青年学生窗下那棵玫瑰树上。

她仍旧叫道："给我一朵红玫瑰，我为你唱最甜美的歌。"

可是那树摇头。

那树回答她道："我的玫瑰是红的，红如白鸽的脚趾，红如海底岩下蠕动的珊瑚。但是严冬已冻僵了我的血脉，寒霜已啮伤了我的萌芽，暴风已打断了我的枝干，今年我不能再开了。"

夜莺央告说："一朵红玫瑰就够了。只要一朵红玫瑰！请问有什么法子没有？"

那树答道："有一个法子，只有一个，但是太可怕了，我不敢告诉你。"

"告诉我吧，"夜莺勇敢地说，"我不怕。"

那树说道："你若要一朵红玫瑰，你须在月色里用音乐制成，然后用你自己的心血染它。你须将胸口顶着一根尖刺为我歌唱。你须整夜地为我歌唱，那刺须刺入你的心头，你生命的血液得流到我的心房里，变成我的血液。"

夜莺叹道："拿死来买一朵红玫瑰，代价真不小。谁的生命不是宝贵的？坐在青郁的森林里，看太阳在黄金马车里，月亮在白珠辇内驰骋，真是一桩乐事。山楂花的味儿真香，山谷里的吊钟花和盛开在山坡上的杜鹃花真美。然而爱比生命更可贵，一个鸟的心又怎能和人的心比？"

忽然她张起棕色的双翼，冲天飞去。如同影子一般穿过那花园，她荡出了那树林。

那青年学生仍旧僵卧在草地上方才她离去的地方，他那双秀眼里的泪珠还没有干。

夜莺喊道："高兴吧，快乐吧！你将要采到你那朵红玫瑰了。我将用月下的歌声制成它。我向你所求的报酬，仅是要你做一个真挚的情人，因为哲理虽智，爱比它更慧，权力虽雄，爱比它更伟。焰光的色彩是爱的双翅，烈火的颜色是爱的躯干。它有如蜜的口唇，若兰的吐气。"

青年学生从草里抬头侧耳静听，但是他不懂夜莺对他所说的话，因他只晓得书上所讲的一切。

那橡树却是懂的，他觉得悲伤，因为他极爱怜那枝上结巢的小夜莺。

他轻声说道："唱一首最后的歌给我听吧，你离去后，我要感到无限的寂寥了。"

于是夜莺为橡树歌唱，她婉转的音调就像在银瓶里涌溢的水浪一般清越。

她唱罢时，那青年学生站起身来从衣袋里抽出一本日记簿和一支笔。

他一面走出那树林，一面自语道："那夜莺的确有些姿态。这是人所不能否认的；但是她有感情吗？我怕没有。实在她就像许多艺术家一般，尽是仪式，没有诚心。她必不肯为人牺牲。她所想的无非是音乐，可是谁不知道艺术是为己的。虽然，我们总须承认她有醉人的歌喉。可惜那种歌声也是无意义，毫无实用的。"于是他回到自己室中，躺在他的小草垫的床上想念他的爱人；过了片时他就睡去了。

待月亮升到天空，放出它的光艳时，那夜莺也就来到玫瑰枝边，将胸口插在刺上。她胸前插着尖刺，整夜地歌唱，那晶莹的月亮倚在云边静听。她整夜地，哳着歌喉，那刺越插越深，她生命的血液渐渐溢出。

最先她歌颂的是稚男幼女心胸里爱恋的诞生。于是那玫瑰的顶尖枝上结了一苞卓绝的玫瑰蕾，歌儿一首连着一首地唱，花瓣一片跟着一片地开。起先那瓣儿是黯淡的，如同河上罩着的薄雾，如同晨曦交际的天色，随后是银灰的，好似曙光的翅翼，那枝上玫瑰蕾就像映在银镜里的玫瑰影子或是照在池塘的玫瑰化身。

但是那树还催迫着夜莺紧插那枝刺。"靠紧那刺，小夜莺。"那树连声地叫唤，"不然，玫瑰还没开成，晓光就要闯来了。"

于是那尖刺插入得越紧，她的歌声越嘹亮，因她这回所歌颂的是成年男女心中热烈如火的爱情。

如今那玫瑰瓣上生了一层娇嫩的红晕，如同初吻新娘时新郎的绛颊。但是那刺还未插到夜莺的心房，所以那花心尚留着白色，因为只有夜莺的心血可以染成玫瑰花心。

那树复催迫着夜莺紧插那枝刺。"靠紧那刺，小夜莺，"那树连声地叫唤，"不然，玫瑰还没开成，晓光就要闯来了。"

于是夜莺紧紧插入那枝刺，那刺居然插入了她的心，但是一种奇痛穿过她的全身，那种惨痛愈猛、愈烈，她的歌声越狂、越壮，因为她这回歌颂的是因死而完成的挚爱和冢中不朽的爱情。

那卓绝的玫瑰于是变作鲜红，如同东方的天色。花的外瓣红如烈火，花的内心赤如绛玉。

夜莺的声音越唱越模糊了，她的双翅拍动起来，她的眼上起了一层薄膜。她的歌声模糊了，她觉得喉间哽咽了。

于是她放出末次的歌声，白色的残月听见，忘记天晓，挂在空中停着。那红玫瑰听见，凝神战栗着，在清冷的晓风里瓣瓣地开放。回声将歌声领入山坡上的紫洞，将牧童从梦里惊醒。歌声流到河边苇丛中，苇叶将这信息传与大海。

那树叫道："看，这玫瑰已制成了。"然而夜莺并不回答，她已躺在乱草里死去，那刺还插在心头。

日午时青年学生开窗向外看。

他叫道："怪事，真是难遇的幸运，这儿有朵红玫瑰，这样的好玫瑰，我生来从没有见过。它这样美丽红艳，定有很繁长的拉丁名字。"说着便俯身下去折了这花。

夜莺与玫瑰

9

于是他戴上帽子，跑到教授家去，手里拈着红玫瑰。

教授的女儿正坐在门前卷一轴蓝色绸子，她的小狗伏在她脚前。

青年学生叫道："你说过我若为你采得红玫瑰，你便同我跳舞。这里有一朵全世界最珍贵的红玫瑰。你可以将她插在你的胸前，我们共舞的时候，这花便能告诉你，我怎样地爱你。"

那女郎只皱着眉头。

她答说："我怕这花不能配上我的衣裳；而且大臣的侄子送我许多珠宝首饰，人人都知道珠宝比花草贵重。"

青年学生怒道："我敢说你是个无情义的人。"他便将玫瑰掷在街心，红玫瑰掉在车辙里，被一个车轮轧过。

女郎说："无情义？我告诉你吧，你实在无礼；况且到底你是谁？不过一个学生文人，我看像大臣侄子鞋上的那银纽扣，你都没有。"说着站起身来走回房去。

青年学生走着自语道："爱，好傻呀，远不如伦理学那般有实用，它所告诉我们的，无非是空中楼阁，实际上不会发生的，和缥缈的虚无不可信的事件。在现实的世界里，首要的是实用，我还是回到我的哲学和玄学书上去吧。"

　　于是他回到房中取出一本笨重的，满堆着尘土的大书埋头细读。

The Nightingale and the Rose

"She said that she would dance with me if I brought her red roses," cried the young Student, "but in all my garden there is no red rose."

From her nest in the holm-oak tree the Nightingale heard him, and she looked out through the leaves and wondered.

"No red rose in all my garden!" he cried, and his beautiful eyes filled with tears. "Ah, on what little things does happiness depend! I have read all that the wise men have written, and all the secrets of philosophy are mine, yet for want of a red rose is my life made wretched."

"Here at last is a true lover," said the Nightingale. "Night after night have I sung of him, though I knew him not: night after night have I told his story to the stars and now I see him. His hair is dark as the hyacinth-blossom, and his lips are red as the rose of his desire;

夜
莺
与
玫
瑰

12

but passion has made his face like pale ivory, and sorrow has set her seal upon his brow."

"The Prince gives a ball tomorrow night," murmured the young Student, "and my love will be of the company. If I bring her a red rose she will dance with me till dawn. If I bring her a red rose, I should hold her in my arms, and she will lean her head upon my shoulder, and her hand will be clasped in mine. But there is no red rose in my garden, so I shall sit lonely, and she will pass me by. She will have no heed of me, and my heart will break."

"Here, indeed, is the true lover," said the Nightingale. "What I sing of, he suffers: what is joy to me, to him is pain. Surely Love is a wonderful thing. It is more precious than emeralds, and dearer than fine opals. Pearls and pomegranates cannot buy it, nor is it set forth in the market-place. It may not be purchased of the merchants, nor can it be weighed out in the balance for gold."

"The musicians will sit in their gallery," said

夜莺与玫瑰

the young Student, "and play upon their stringed instruments, and my love will dance to the sound of the harp and the violin. She will dance so lightly that her feet will not touch the floor, and the courtiers in their gay dresses will throng round her. But with me she will not dance, for I have no red rose to give her;" and he flung himself down on the grass, and buried his face in his hands, and wept.

"Why is he weeping?" asked a little Green Lizard, as he ran past him with his tail in the air.

"Why, indeed?" said a Butterfly, who was fluttering about after a sunbeam.

"Why, indeed?" whispered a Daisy to his neighbour, in a soft, low voice.

"He is weeping for a red rose," said the Nightingale.

"For a red rose?" they cried; "how very ridiculous!" and the little Lizard, who was something of a cynic, laughed outright.

But the Nightingale understood the secret of the Student's sorrow, and she sat silent in the oak-tree, and thought about the mystery of Love.

Suddenly she spread her brown wings for flight, and soared into the air. She passed through the grove like a shadow and like a shadow she sailed across the garden.

In the center of the grass-plot was standing a beautiful Rose-tree, and when she saw it she flew over to it, and lit upon a spray.

"Give me a red rose," she cried, "and I will sing you my sweetest song."

But the Tree shook its head.

"My roses are white," it answered; "as white as the foam of the sea, and whiter than the snow upon the mountain. But go to my brother who grows round the old sun-dial, and perhaps he will give you what you want."

So the Nightingale flew over to the Rose-tree that was growing round the old sun-dial.

"Give me a red rose," she cried, "and I will sing you my sweetest song."

夜莺与玫瑰

15

But the Tree shook its head.

"My roses are yellow," it answered; "as yellow as the hair of the mermaiden who sits upon an amber throne, and yellower than the daffodil that blooms in the meadow before the mower comes with his scythe. But go to my brother who grows beneath the Student's window, and perhaps he will give you what you want."

So the Nightingale flew over to the Rose-tree that was growing beneath the Student's window.

"Give me a red rose," she cried, "and I will sing you my sweetest song."

But the Tree shook its head.

"My roses are red," it answered, "as red as the feet of the dove, and redder than the great fans of coral that wave and wave in the ocean-cavern. But the winter has chilled my veins, and the frost has nipped my buds, and the storm has broken my branches, and I shall have no roses at all this year."

"One red rose is all I want," cried the Nightingale,

"only one red rose! Is there no way by which I can get it?"

"There is a way," answered the Tree; "but it is so terrible that I dare not tell it to you."

"Tell it to me," said the Nightingale, "I am not afraid."

"If you want a red rose," said the Tree, "you must build it out of music by moonlight, and stain it with your own heart's blood. You must sing to me with your breast against a thorn. All night long you must sing to me, and the thorn must pierce your heart, and your life-blood must flow into my veins, and become mine."

"Death is a great price to pay for a red rose," cried the Nightingale, "and Life is very dear to all. It is pleasant to sit in the green wood, and to watch the Sun in his chariot of gold, and the Moon in her chariot of pearl. Sweet is the scent of the hawthorn, and sweet are the bluebells that hide in the valley, and the heather that blows on the hill. Yet Love is better than Life, and what is the heart of a bird compared to the

夜莺与玫瑰

heart of a man?"

So she spread her brown wings for flight, and soared into the air. She swept over the garden like a shadow, and like a shadow she sailed through the grove.

The young Student was still lying on the grass, where she had left him, and the tears were not yet dry in his beautiful eyes.

"Be happy," cried the Nightingale, "be happy; you shall have your red rose. I will build it out of music by moonlight, and stain it with my own heart's blood. All that I ask of you in return is that you will be a true lover, for Love is wiser than Philosophy, though he is wise, and mightier than Power, though he is mighty. Flame-coloured are his wings, and coloured like flame is his body. His lips are sweet as honey, and his breath is like frankincense."

The Student looked up from the grass, and listened, but he could not understand what the Nightingale was saying to him, for he only knew the things that are

夜
莺
与
玫
瑰

written down in books.

But the Oak-tree understood, and felt sad, for he was very fond of the little Nightingale, who had built her nest in his branches.

"Sing me one last song," he whispered; "I shall feel lonely when you are gone."

So the Nightingale sang to the Oak-tree, and her voice was like water bubbling from a silver jar.

When she had finished her song, the Student got up, and pulled a note-book and a lead-pencil out of his pocket.

"She had form," he said to himself, as he walked away through the grove—"that cannot be denied to her; but has she got feeling? I am afraid not. In fact, she is like most artists; she is all style without any sincerity. She would not sacrifice herself for others. She thinks merely of music, and everybody knows that the arts are selfish. Still, it must be admitted that she has some beautiful notes in her voice. What a pity it is that they do not mean anything, or do any practical good!" And

夜莺与玫瑰

19

he went into his room, and lay down on his little pallet-bed, and began to think of his love; and, after a time, he fell asleep.

And when the Moon shone in the heavens the Nightingale flew to the Rose-tree, and set her breast against the thorn. All night long she sang, with her breast against the thorn, and the cold crystal Moon leaned down and listened. All night long she sang, and the thorn went deeper and deeper into her breast, and her life-blood ebbed away from her.

She sang first of the birth of love in the heart of a boy and a girl. And on the topmost spray of the Rose-tree there blossomed a marvelous rose, petal following petal, as song followed song. Pale was it, at first, as the mist that hangs over the river—pale as the feet of the morning, and silver as the wings of the dawn. As the shadow of a rose in a mirror of silver, as the shadow of a rose in a water-pool, so was the rose that blossomed on the topmost spray of the Tree.

夜
莺
与
玫
瑰

But the Tree cried to the Nightingale to press closer against the thorn. "Press closer, little Nightingale," cried the Tree, "or the Day will come before the rose is finished."

So the Nightingale's pressed closer against the thorn, and louder and louder grew her song, for she sang of the birth of passion in the soul of a man and a maid.

And a delicate flush of pink came into the leaves of the rose, like the flush in the face of the bridegroom when he kisses the lips of the bride. But the thorn had not yet reached her heart, so the rose's heart remained white, for only a Nightingale's heart's blood can crimson the heart of a rose.

And the Tree cried to the Nightingale to press closer against the thorn. "Press closer, little Nightingale," cried the Tree, "or the Day will come before the rose is finished."

So the Nightingale pressed closer against the thorn, and the thorn touched her heart, and a fierce pang of

夜莺与玫瑰

pain shot through her. Bitter, bitter was the pain, and wilder and wilder grew her song, for she sang of the Love that is perfected by Death, of the Love that dies not in the tomb.

And the marvelous rose became crimson, like the rose of the eastern sky. Crimson was the girdle of petals, and crimson as a ruby was the heart.

But the Nightingale's voice grew fainter, and her little wings began to beat, and a film came over her eyes. Fainter and fainter grew her song, and she felt something choking her in her throat.

Then she gave one last burst of music. The white Moon heard it, and she forgot the dawn, and lingered on in the sky. The red rose heard it, and it trembled all over with ecstasy, and opened its petals to the cold morning air. Echo bore it to her purple cavern in the hills, and woke the sleeping shepherds from their dreams. It floated through the reeds of the river, and they carried its message to the sea.

"Look, look!" cried the Tree, "the rose is finished

夜
莺
与
玫
瑰

now;" but the Nightingale made not answer, for she was lying dead in the long grass, with the thorn in her heart.

And at noon the Student opened his window and looked out.

"Why, what a wonderful piece of luck!" He cried; "here is a red rose! I have never seen any rose like it in all my life. It is so beautiful that I am sure it has a long Latin name;" and he leaned down and plucked it.

Then he put on his hat, and ran up to the Professor's house with the rose in his hand.

The daughter of the Professor was sitting in the doorway winding blue silk on a reel, and her little dog was lying at her feet.

"You said that you would dance with me if I brought you a red rose," cried the Student. "Here is the reddest rose in all the world. You will wear it tonight next your heart, and as we dance together it will tell you how I love you."

But the girl frowned.

夜莺与玫瑰

"I am afraid it will not go with my dress," she answered; "and, besides, the Chamberlain's nephew had sent me some real jewels, and everybody knows that jewels cost far more than flowers."

"Well, upon my word, you are very ungrateful," said the Student angrily; and he threw the rose onto the street, where it fell into the gutter, and a cart-wheel went over it.

"Ungrateful!" said the girl. "I tell you what, you are very rude; and, after all, who are you? Only a Student. Why, I don't believe you have even got silver buckles to your shoes as the Chamberlain's nephew has;" and she got up from her chair and went into the house.

"What a silly thing Love is!" said the Student as he walked away. "It is not half as useful as Logic, for it does not prove anything, and it is always telling one of things that are not going to happen, and making one believe things that are not true. In fact, it is quite unpractical, and, as in this age to be practical is everything, I shall go back to Philosophy and study Metaphysics."

So he returned to his room and pulled out a great dusty book, and began to read.

快乐王子

快乐王子的雕像高高地耸立在城市上空一根高大的石柱上面。他浑身上下镶满了薄薄的黄金叶片，明亮的蓝宝石做成他的双眼，剑柄上还嵌着一颗硕大的灿灿发光的红宝石。

世人对他真是钦慕不已。"他像风向标一样漂亮，"一位想表现自己有艺术品位的市参议员说了一句，接着又担心人们将他视为不务实际的人，其实他倒是怪务实的，便补充道，"只是不如风向标那么实用。"

"你为什么不能像快乐王子一样呢？"一位明智的母亲对自己那哭喊着要月亮的小男孩说，"快乐王子做梦时都从没有想过哭着要东西。"

"世上还有如此快乐的人，真让我高兴。"一位沮丧的汉子凝视着这座非凡的雕像喃喃自语。

"他看上去就像位天使。"孤儿院的孩子们说。他们正从教堂走出来，身上披着鲜红夺目的斗篷，胸前挂着干净雪白的围嘴儿。

"你们是怎么知道的？"数学教师问道，"你们又没见过天使的模样。"

"啊！我们见过，是在梦里见到的。"孩子们答道。数学教师皱皱眉头并绷起了面孔，因为他不赞成孩子们做梦。

有一天夜里，一只小燕子从城市上空飞过。他的朋友们早在六个星期前就飞往埃及去了，可他却落在了后面，因为他太留恋那美丽无比的芦苇小姐。他是在早春时节遇上她的，当时他正顺河而下去追逐一只黄色的大飞蛾。他为她那纤细的腰身着了迷，便停下身来同她说话。

"我可以爱你吗？"小燕子问道，他喜欢一下子就谈到正题上。芦苇向他弯下了腰，于是他就绕着她飞了一圈又一圈，并用翅膀轻盈地点水，撩起层层银色的涟漪。这是小燕子的求爱方式，他就这样过了整个夏天。

"这种恋情实在可笑，"其他小燕子嘲笑他，"她既没钱财，又有那么多亲戚。"的确，河里到处都是芦苇。等秋天一到，小燕子们就飞走了。

大伙儿走后，他觉得很孤独，并开始讨厌自己的恋人。"她不会说话，"他说，"况且我担心她是个荡妇，你看她老是跟风调情。"这可不假，一旦起风，芦苇便行起最优雅的屈膝礼。"我承认她是个居家过日子的人，"小燕子继续说，"可我喜爱旅行，而我的妻子，当然也应该喜爱旅行才对。"

"你愿意跟我走吗？"他最后问道。然而芦苇却摇摇头，她太舍不得自己的家了。

"原来你跟我是闹着玩儿的，"他吼叫着，"我要去金字塔了，再见吧！"说完他就飞走了。

他飞了整整一天，夜晚时才来到这座城市。"我去哪儿过夜呢？"他说，"我希望在这座城里找到栖身之地。"

这时，他看见了高大圆柱上的雕像。

"我就在那儿过夜，"他高声说，"这是个好地方，空气新鲜。"于是，他就在快乐王子两脚之间做了窝。

"我有黄金做的卧室。"他朝四周看看，轻声地对自己说，随之准备入睡了。但就在他把头放在羽翅下面的时候，一颗大大的水珠落在他的身上。"真是不可思议！"他叫了起来，"天上没有一丝云彩，繁星清晰又明亮，却偏偏下起了雨。北欧的天气真是可怕。芦苇也是喜欢雨水的，可那只是她自私罢了。"

紧接着又落下来一滴。

"一座雕像连雨都遮挡不住，还有什么用处？"他说，"我得去找一个好烟囱做窝。"他决定飞走。

可是还没等他张开羽翼，第三滴水又掉了下来，他抬头望去，看见了——啊！他看见了什么呢？

快乐王子的双眼充满了泪水，泪珠顺着他金黄的脸颊淌了下来。王子的脸在月光下美丽无比，小燕子顿生怜悯之心。

"你是谁？"小燕子问。

"我是快乐王子。"

"那么你为什么哭呢？"小燕子又问，"你把我的身上都打湿了。"

"当我还活着，还有一颗属于人的心时，"雕像开口说道，"我并不知道眼泪是什么东西，因为那时我住在逍遥自在的王宫里，那是个哀愁无法进去的地方。白天人们伴着我在花园里玩，晚上我在大厅里领头跳舞。沿着

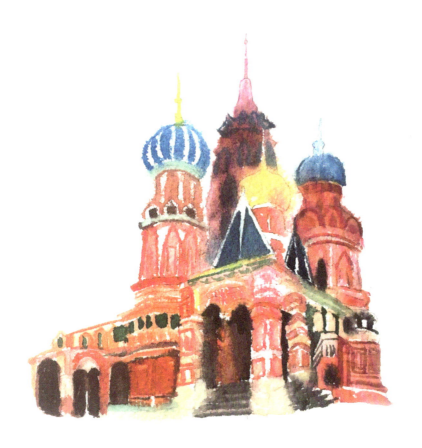

花园有一堵高高的围墙，可我从没想到去问墙那边有什
么东西，我身边的一切太美好了。我的臣仆们都叫我快
乐王子，的确，如果欢愉就是快乐的话，那我真是快乐
无比。我就这么活着，也这么死去。而眼下我死了，他
们把我这么高高地立在这儿，使我能看见自己城市中所
有的丑恶和贫苦，尽管我的心是铅做的，可我还是忍不
住要哭。"

"啊！难道他不是纯金的？"小燕子对自己说。他很
讲礼貌，不愿大声议论别人的私事。

"远处，"雕像用低缓而悦耳的声音继续说，"远处的一条小街上住着一户穷人。一扇窗户开着，透过窗户我能看见一个女人坐在桌旁。她那瘦削的脸上布满了倦意，一双粗糙发红的手上到处是被针扎伤的痕迹，因为她是一个裁缝。她正在给缎子衣服绣上西番莲，这是皇后最喜爱的宫女准备在下一次宫廷舞会上穿的。在房间角落里的一张床上躺着她生病的孩子。孩子在发热，嚷着要吃橘子。他的妈妈除给他喂几口河水外什么也没有，因此孩子老是哭个不停。燕子，燕子，小燕子，你愿意把我剑柄上的红宝石取下来送给她吗？我的双脚被固定在这基座上，不能动。"

　　"伙伴们在埃及等我，"小燕子说，"他们正在尼罗河上飞来飞去，同朵朵大莲花说着话，不久就要到伟大法老的墓穴里去过夜。法老本人就睡在自己彩色的棺材中。他的身体被裹在黄色的亚麻布里，还填满了防腐的香料。他的脖子上系着一圈浅绿色翡翠项链，他的双手像是枯萎的树叶。"

　　"燕子，燕子，小燕子，"王子又说，"你不肯陪我过一夜，做我的信使吗？那个孩子太饥渴了，他的母亲伤心极了。"

"我觉得自己不喜欢小孩，"小燕子回答说，"去年夏天，我到过一条河边，有两个顽皮的孩子，是磨坊主的儿子，他们老是扔石头打我。当然，他们永远也别想打中我，我们燕子飞得多快呀，再说，我祖上都善于飞翔；可不管怎么说，这是不礼貌的行为。"

　　可是快乐王子的满脸愁容叫小燕子的心里很不好受。"这儿太冷了，"他说，"不过我愿意陪你过上一夜，并做你的信使。"

　　"谢谢你，小燕子。"王子说。

于是小燕子从王子的宝剑上取下那颗硕大的红宝石，用嘴衔着，越过城里一座连一座的屋顶，朝远方飞去。

他飞过大教堂的塔顶，看见了上面白色大理石雕刻的天使像。他飞过王宫，听见了跳舞的乐声。一位美丽的姑娘同她的心上人走上了天台。"多么奇妙的星星啊，"男子对姑娘说，"多么美妙的爱情啊。"

"我希望我的衣服能按时做好，赶得上盛大舞会，"姑娘回答说，"我已要求绣上西番莲，只是那些女裁缝们都太懒了。"

他飞过了河流，看见了高挂在船桅上的无数灯笼。他飞过了犹太区，看见犹太老人们在彼此讨价还价地做生意，还把钱币放在铜制的天平上称重量。最后他来到了那个穷人的屋舍，朝里面望去。发热的孩子在床上辗转反侧，母亲已经睡熟了，因为她太疲倦了。他跳进屋里，将硕大的红宝石放在那女人顶针旁的桌子上。随后他又轻轻地绕着床飞了一圈，用翅膀扇着孩子的前额。"我觉得好凉爽，"孩子说，"我一定是好起来了。"说完就沉沉地进入了甜蜜的梦乡。

然后，小燕子回到快乐王子的身边，告诉他自己做过的一切。"你说怪不怪，"他接着说，"虽然天气很冷，可我现在觉得好暖和。"

　　"那是因为你做了一件好事，"王子说。于是小燕子开始想王子的话，不过没多久便睡着了。对他来说，一思考问题就老想睡觉。

　　黎明时分他飞下河去洗了个澡。"真是不可思议的现象，"一位鸟类学家从桥上走过时说道，"冬天竟会有燕子！"于是他把这事写成一封长信，寄给了当地的报社。每个人都引用他信中的话，尽管信中的很多词语是人们理解不了的。

　　"今晚我要到埃及去。"小燕子说，一想到远方，他就精神百倍。他走访了城里所有的公共纪念碑，还在教堂的顶端坐了好一阵子。每到一处，麻雀们就叽叽喳喳地相互说："多么难得的贵客啊！"所以他玩得很开心。

　　月亮升起的时候他飞回到快乐王子的身边。"你在埃及有什么事要办吗？"他高声问道，"我就要动身了。"

　　"燕子，燕子，小燕子，"王子说，"你愿意陪我再过一夜吗？"

　　"伙伴们在埃及等我呀，"小燕子回答说，"明天我的朋友们要飞往第二瀑布，那儿的河马在纸莎草丛中过夜。古埃及的孟农神安坐在巨大的花岗岩宝座上，他整夜守

夜莺与玫瑰

望着星星，每当晨星闪烁的时候，他就发出欢快的叫声，随后便沉默不语。中午时，黄色的狮群下山来到河边饮水，他们的眼睛像绿色的宝石，咆哮起来比瀑布的怒吼还要响亮。"

"燕子，燕子，小燕子，"王子说，"远处在城市的那一头，我看见住在阁楼中的一个年轻男子。他在一张铺满纸张的书桌上埋头用功，旁边的玻璃杯中放着一束干枯的紫罗兰。他有一头棕色的卷发，嘴唇红得像石榴，他还有一双睡意蒙眬的大眼睛。他正力争为剧院经理写出一个剧本，但是他已经被冻得写不下去了。壁炉里没有柴火，饥饿又弄得他头昏眼花。"

"我愿意陪你再过一夜，"小燕子说，他的确有颗善良的心。"我是不是再送他一块红宝石？"

"唉！我现在没有红宝石了。"王子说，"所剩的只有我的双眼。它们由稀有的蓝宝石做成，是一千多年前从印度出产的。取出一颗给他送去。他会将它卖给珠宝商，买回食物和木柴，完成他写的剧本。"

"亲爱的王子，"小燕子说，"我不能这样做。"说完就哭了起来。

"燕子，燕子，小燕子，"王子说，"就照我说的话去做吧。"

因此小燕子取下了王子的一只眼睛，朝男子住的阁楼飞去了。由于屋顶上有一个洞，小燕子很容易进去。就这样小燕子穿过洞来到屋里。年轻男子双手捂着脸，没有听见小燕子翅膀的扇动声，等他抬起头时，正看见那颗美丽的蓝宝石放在干枯的紫罗兰上面。

"我开始受人欣赏了，"他叫道，"这准是某个极其钦佩我的人送来的。现在我可以完成我的剧本了。"他脸上露出了幸福的笑容。

第二天小燕子飞到下面的海港，他坐在一艘大船的桅杆上，望着水手们用绳索把大箱子拖出船舱。随着他们"嘿哟！嘿哟！"的声声号子，一个个大箱子被拖了上来。"我要去埃及了！"小燕子说，但是没有人理会他。等月亮升起后，他又飞回到快乐王子的身边。

"我是来向你道别的。"他叫着说。

"燕子，燕子，小燕子，"王子说，"你不愿再陪我过一夜吗？"

"冬天到了，"小燕子回答说，"寒冷的雪就要来了。而在埃及，太阳挂在葱绿的棕榈树上，暖和极了，躺在泥塘中的鳄鱼懒洋洋地环顾着四周。我的朋友们正在太阳城的神庙里建筑巢穴，那些粉红和银色的鸽子们一边望着他们干活，一边相互倾诉着情话。亲爱的王子，我不得不离你而去了，只是我永远也不会忘记你的，明年春天我要给你带回两颗美丽的宝石，弥补你因送给别人而失掉的那两颗，红宝石会比红玫瑰还红，蓝宝石也比大海更蓝。"

"在下面的广场上，"快乐王子说，"站着一个卖火柴的小女孩。她的火柴都掉在阴沟里了，它们都不能用了。如果她不带钱回家，她的父亲会打她的，她正在哭呢。她既没穿鞋，也没有穿袜子，头上什么也没戴。请把我的另一只眼睛取下来，给她送去，这样她父亲就不会揍她了。"

"我愿意陪你再过一夜，"小燕子说，"但我不能取下你的眼睛，否则你就变成个瞎子了。"

"燕子，燕子，小燕子，"王子说，"就照我说的话去做吧。"

于是他又取下了王子的另一只眼睛，带着它朝下飞去。他一下子落在小女孩的面前，把宝石悄悄地放在她的手掌心里。"一块多么美丽的玻璃呀！"小女孩高声叫着，她笑着朝家里跑去。

这时，小燕子回到王子身旁。"你现在瞎了，"小燕子说，"我要永远陪着你。"

"不，小燕子，"可怜的王子说，"你得到埃及去。"

"我要一直陪着你。"小燕子说着就睡在了王子的脚下。

第二天，他整日坐在王子的肩头上，给他讲自己在异国他乡的所见所闻和种种经历。他还给王子讲那些红色的朱鹮，它们排成长长的一行站在尼罗河的岸边，用它们的尖嘴去捕捉金鱼；还讲到斯芬克斯，它的岁数跟世界一样长久，住在沙漠中，通晓世间的一切；他讲到那些商人，跟着自己的骆驼队缓缓而行，手中摸着琥珀珠；他讲到月亮山的国王，他皮肤黑得像乌木，崇拜一块巨大的水晶；他讲到那条睡在棕榈树上的绿色大蟒蛇，要20个僧侣用蜜糖做的糕点来喂它；他又讲到那些小矮人，他们乘坐扁平的大树叶在湖泊中往来横渡，还老与蝴蝶发生战争。

"亲爱的小燕子，"王子说，"你为我讲了好多稀奇的事情，可是更稀奇的还要算那些男男女女们所遭受的苦难。没有什么比苦难更不可思议的了。小燕子，你就到我城市的上空去飞一圈吧，告诉我你在上面都看见了些什么。"

于是小燕子飞过了城市上空，看见富人们在自己漂亮的洋楼里寻欢作乐，而乞丐们却坐在大门口忍饥挨饿。他飞进阴暗的小巷，看见饥饿的孩子们露出苍白的小脸，没精打采地望着昏暗的街道。就在一座桥的桥洞里面，两个孩子相互搂抱着想使彼此温暖一些。"我们好饿呀！"他俩说。"你们不准躺在这儿。"看守高声喊道，两个孩子又蹒跚着朝雨中走去。

随后他飞了回来，把所见的一切告诉给了王子。

"我浑身贴满了上好的黄金片，"王子说，"你把它们一片片地取下来，给我的穷人们送去。活着的人都相信黄金会使自己幸福。"

小燕子将黄金叶子一片一片地啄了下来，直到快乐王子变得灰暗无光。他又把这些纯金叶片一一送给了穷人，孩子们的脸上泛起了红晕，他们在大街上欢欣无比地玩着游戏。"我们现在有面包了！"孩子们喊叫着。

随后下起了雪，白雪过后又迎来了严寒。街道看上去白花花的，像是银子做成的，又明亮又耀眼；长长的冰柱如同水晶做的宝剑垂悬在屋檐下。人人都穿上了皮衣，小孩子们也戴上了红帽子去户外溜冰。

可怜的小燕子觉得越来越冷了，但是他却不愿离开王子，他太爱这位王子了。他只好趁面包师不注意的时候，从面包店门口弄点面包屑充饥，并拍打着翅膀为自己取暖。

然而最后他也知道自己快要死去。他剩下的力气只够再飞到王子的肩上一回。"再见了，亲爱的王子！"他喃喃地说，"你愿意让我亲吻你的手吗？"

"我真高兴你终于要飞往埃及去了，小燕子，"王子说，"你在这儿待得太长了。不过你得亲我的嘴唇，因为我爱你。"

"我要去的地方不是埃及，"小燕子说，"我要奔向死亡。死亡是长眠的兄弟，不是吗？"

接着他亲吻了快乐王子的嘴唇，然后就跌落在王子的脚下，死去了。

就在此刻，雕像体内发出一声奇特的爆裂声，好像有什么东西破碎了。其实是王子的那颗铅做的心已裂成了两半。这的确是一个可怕的寒冷冬日。

第二天一早，市长由市参议员们陪同着散步来到下面的广场。他们走过圆柱的时候，市长抬头看了一眼雕像，"我的天啊！快乐王子怎么如此难看！"他说。

"真是难看极了！"市参议员们异口同声地叫道，他们平时总跟市长一个腔调。说完大家纷纷走上前去细看个明白。

"他剑柄上的红宝石已经掉了，蓝宝石眼睛也不见了，他也不再是黄金的了，"市长说，"实际上，他比一个要饭的乞丐强不了多少！"

"的确比要饭的强不了多少。"市参议员们附和着说。

"还有，在他的脚下躺着一只死鸟！"市长继续说，"我们真应该发布一个声明，禁止鸟类死在这个地方。"于是市书记员把这个建议记录了下来。

后来他们就把快乐王子的雕像给推倒了。"既然他已不再美丽，那么也就不再有用了。"大学的美术教授说。

接着他们把雕像放在炉里熔化了，市长还召集了一次市级的会议来决定如何处理这些金属，"当然，我们必须再铸一个雕像。"他说，"那应该就是我的雕像。"

"我的雕像。"每一位市参议员都争着说，他们还吵了起来。

"多么稀奇古怪的事！"铸像厂的工头说，"这颗破裂的铅心在炉子里熔化不了。我们只好把它扔掉。"他们便把它扔到了垃圾堆里，死去的那只小燕子也躺在那儿。

"把城市里最珍贵的两件东西给我拿来。"上帝对他的一位天使说。于是天使就把铅心和死鸟给上帝带了回来。

　　"你的选择对极了，"上帝说，"因为在我这天堂的花园里，小鸟可以永远地放声歌唱，而在我那黄金的城堡中，快乐王子可以尽情地赞美我。"

The Happy Prince

High above the city, on a tall column, stood the statue of the Happy Prince. He was gilded all over with thin leaves of fine gold, for eyes he had two bright sapphires, and a large red ruby glowed on his sword-hilt.

He was very much admired indeed. "He is as beautiful as a weathercock," remarked one of the Town Councillors who wished to gain a reputation for having artistic tastes; "only not quite so useful," he added, fearing lest people should think him unpractical, which he really was not.

"Why can't you be like the Happy Prince?" asked a sensible mother of her little boy who was crying for the moon. "The Happy Prince never dreams of crying for anything."

"I am glad there is someone in the world who is quite happy," muttered a disappointed man as he

快
乐
王
子

gazed at the wonderful statue.

"He looks just like an angel," said the Charity Children as they came out of the cathedral in their bright scarlet cloaks and their clean white pinafores.

"How do you know?" said the Mathematical Master, "you have never seen one."

"Ah! But we have, in our dreams," answered the children; and the Mathematical Master frowned and looked very severe, for he did not approve of children dreaming.

One night there flew over the city a little Swallow. His friends had gone away to Egypt six weeks before, but he had stayed behind, for he was in love with the most beautiful Reed. He had met her early in the spring as he was flying down the river after a big yellow moth, and had been so attracted by her slender waist that he had stopped to talk to her.

"Shall I love you?" said the Swallow, who liked to come to the point at once, and the Reed made him a low bow. So he flew round and round her, touching the water with his wings, and making silver ripples. This was his courtship, and it lasted all through the summer.

"It is a ridiculous attachment," twittered the other Swallows; "she has no money, and far too many relations;" and indeed the river was quite full of Reeds. Then, when the autumn came they all flew away.

After they had gone he felt lonely, and began to tire of his lady-love. "She has no conversation," he said, "and I am afraid that she is a coquette, for she is always flirting with the wind." And certainly, whenever the wind blew, the Reed made the most graceful curtseys. "I admit that she is domestic," he continued, "but I love travelling, and my wife, consequently, should love travelling also."

"Will you come away with me?" he said finally to her; but the Reed shook her head, she was so attached to her home.

"You have been trifling with me," he cried. "I am off to the Pyramids. Good-bye!" and he flew away.

All day long he flew, and at night-time he arrived at the city. "Where shall I put up?" he said; "I hope the town has made preparations."

Then he saw the statue on the tall column.

"I will put up there," he cried; "it is a fine position, with plenty of fresh air." So he alighted just between the feet of the Happy Prince.

"I have a golden bedroom," he said softly to himself as he looked round, and he prepared to go to sleep; but just as he was putting his head under his wing a large drop of water fell on him. "What a curious thing!" he cried; "there is not a single cloud in the sky, the stars are quite clear and bright, and yet it is raining. The climate in the north of Europe is really dreadful. The Reed used to like the rain, but that was merely her selfishness."

Then another drop fell.

"What is the use of a statue if it cannot keep the

rain off?" he said; "I must look for a good chimney-pot," and he determined to fly away.

But before he had opened his wings, a third drop fell, and he looked up, and saw——Ah! What did he see?

The eyes of the Happy Prince were filled with tears, and tears were running down his golden cheeks. His face was so beautiful in the moonlight that the little Swallow was filled with pity.

"Who are you?" he said.

"I am the Happy Prince."

"Why are you weeping then?" asked the Swallow; "you have quite drenched me."

"When I was alive and had a human heart," answered the statue, "I did not know what tears were, for I lived in the Palace of Sans-Souci, where sorrow is not allowed to enter. In the daytime I played with my companions in the garden, and in the evening I led the dance in the Great Hall. Round the garden ran a very lofty wall, but I never cared to ask what lay beyond it, everything about me was so beautiful. My courtiers called me the Happy Prince, and happy indeed I was, if pleasure be happiness. So I lived, and so I died. And now that I am dead they have set me up here so high that I can see all the ugliness and all the misery of my city, and though my heart is made of lead yet I cannot chose but weep."

"What! Is he not solid gold?" said the Swallow to himself. He was too polite to make any personal remarks out loud.

"Far away," continued the statue in a low musical voice, "far away in a little street there is a poor house. One of the windows is open, and through it I can see a woman seated at a table. Her face is thin and worn, and she has coarse, red hands, all pricked by the needle, for she is a seamstress. She is embroidering passion-flowers on a satin gown for the loveliest of the Queen's maids-of-honour to wear at the next Court-ball. In a bed in the corner of the room her little boy is lying ill. He has a fever, and is asking for oranges. His mother has nothing to give him but river water, so he is crying. Swallow, Swallow, little Swallow, will you not bring her the ruby out of my sword-hilt? My feet are fastened to this pedestal and I cannot move."

"I am waited for in Egypt," said the Swallow. "My friends are flying up and down the Nile, and talking to the large lotus-flowers. Soon they will go to sleep in the tomb of the great King. The King is there himself in his painted coffin. He is wrapped in yellow linen, and embalmed with spices. Round his neck is a chain of pale green jade, and his hands are like withered leaves."

"Swallow, Swallow, little Swallow," said the Prince, "will you not stay with me for one night, and be my messenger? The boy is so thirsty, and the mother so sad."

"I don't think I like boys," answered the Swallow. "Last summer, when I was staying on the river, there were two rude boys, the miller's sons, who were always throwing stones at me. They never hit me, of course; we swallows fly far too well for that, and besides, I come of a family famous for its agility; but still, it was a mark of disrespect."

But the Happy Prince looked so sad that the little Swallow was sorry. "It is very cold here," he said; "but I will stay with you for one night, and be your messenger."

"Thank you, little Swallow," said the Prince.

So the Swallow picked out the great ruby from the Prince's sword, and flew away with it in his beak over the roofs of the town.

He passed by the cathedral tower, where the white marble angels were sculptured. He passed by the palace and heard the sound of dancing. A beautiful girl came out on the balcony with her lover. "How wonderful the stars are," he said to her, "and how wonderful is the power of love!"

"I hope my dress will be ready in time for

the State-ball," she answered; "I have ordered passion-flowers to be embroidered on it; but the seamstresses are so lazy."

He passed over the river, and saw the lanterns hanging to the masts of the ships. He passed over the Ghetto, and saw the old Jews bargaining with each other, and weighing out money in copper scales. At last he came to the poor house and looked in. The boy was tossing feverishly on his bed, and the mother had fallen asleep, she was so tired. In he hopped, and laid the great ruby on the table beside the woman's thimble. Then he flew gently round the bed, fanning the boy's forehead with his wings. "How cool I feel," said the boy, "I must be getting better;" and he sank into a delicious slumber.

Then the Swallow flew back to the Happy Prince, and told him what he had done. "It is curious," he remarked, "but I feel quite warm now, although it is so cold."

"That is because you have done a good action,"

said the Prince. And the little Swallow began to think, and then he fell asleep. Thinking always made him sleepy.

When day broke he flew down to the river and had a bath. "What a remarkable phenomenon," said the Professor of Ornithology as he was passing over the bridge. "A swallow in winter!" And he wrote a long letter about it to the local newspaper. Every one quoted it, it was full of so many words that they could not understand.

"Tonight I go to Egypt," said the Swallow, and he was in high spirits at the prospect. He visited all the public monuments, and sat a long time on top of the church steeple. Wherever he went the Sparrows chirruped, and said to each other, "What a distinguished stranger!" so he enjoyed himself very much.

When the moon rose he flew back to the Happy Prince. "Have you any commissions for Egypt?" he cried; "I am just starting."

"Swallow, Swallow, little Swallow," said the Prince, "will you not stay with me one night longer?"

"I am waited for in Egypt," answered the Swallow. "Tomorrow my friends will fly up to the Second Cataract. The river-horse couches there among the bulrushes, and on a great granite throne sits the God Memnon. All night long he watches the stars, and when the morning star shines he utters one cry of joy, and then he is silent. At noon the yellow lions come down to the water's edge to drink. They have eyes like green beryls, and their roar is louder than the roar of the cataract."

"Swallow, Swallow, little Swallow," said the Prince, "far away across the city I see a young man in a garret. He is leaning over a desk covered with papers, and in a tumbler by his side there is a bunch of withered violets. His hair is brown and crisp, and his lips are red as a pomegranate, and he has large and dreamy eyes. He is trying to finish a play for the Director of the Theatre, but he is too cold to write

快
乐
王
子

any more. There is no fire in the grate, and hunger has made him faint."

"I will wait with you one night longer," said the Swallow, who really had a good heart. "Shall I take him another ruby?"

"Alas! I have no ruby now," said the Prince; "my eyes are all that I have left. They are made of rare sapphires, which were brought out of India a thousand years ago. Pluck out one of them and take it to him. He will sell it to the jeweller, and buy food and firewood, and finish his play."

"Dear Prince," said the Swallow, "I cannot do that;" and he began to weep.

"Swallow, Swallow, little Swallow," said the Prince, "do as I command you."

So the Swallow plucked out the Prince's eye, and flew away to the student's garret. It was easy enough to get in, as there was a hole in the roof. Through this he darted, and came into the room. The young man had his head buried in his hands, so he

夜
莺
与
玫
瑰

did not hear the flutter of the bird's wings, and when he looked up he found the beautiful sapphire lying on the withered violets.

"I am beginning to be appreciated," he cried; "this is from some great admirer. Now I can finish my play," and he looked quite happy.

The next day the Swallow flew down to the harbour. He sat on the mast of a large vessel and watched the sailors hauling big chests out of the hold with ropes. "Heave a-hoy!" they shouted as each chest came up. "I am going to Egypt"! cried the Swallow, but nobody minded, and when the moon rose he flew back to the Happy Prince.

"I am come to bid you good-bye," he cried.

"Swallow, Swallow, little Swallow," said the Prince, "will you not stay with me one night longer?"

"It is winter," answered the Swallow, "and the chill snow will soon be here. In Egypt the sun is warm on the green palm-trees, and the crocodiles lie in the mud and look lazily about them. My companions are building a nest in the Temple of Baalbec[1], and the pink and white doves are watching them, and cooing to each other. Dear Prince, I must leave you, but I will never forget you, and next spring I will bring you back two beautiful jewels in place of those you have given away. The ruby shall be redder than a red rose, and the sapphire shall be as blue as the great sea."

"In the square below," said the Happy Prince, "there stands a little match-girl. She has let her matches fall in the gutter, and they are all spoiled. Her father will beat her if she does not bring home some money, and she is crying. She has no shoes or stockings, and her little head is bare. Pluck out my other eye, and give it to her, and her father will not beat her."

"I will stay with you one night longer," said the

夜 莺 与 玫 瑰

● Baalbec 古希腊语，太阳城。太阳城是古埃及城市，现为开罗所在地。

Swallow, "but I cannot pluck out your eye. You would be quite blind then."

"Swallow, Swallow, little Swallow," said the Prince, "do as I command you."

So he plucked out the Prince's other eye, and darted down with it. He swooped past the match-girl, and slipped the jewel into the palm of her hand. "What a lovely bit of glass," cried the little girl; and she ran home, laughing.

Then the Swallow came back to the Prince. "You are blind now," he said, "so I will stay with you always."

"No, little Swallow," said the poor Prince, "you must go away to Egypt."

"I will stay with you always," said the Swallow, and he slept at the Prince's feet.

All the next day he sat on the Prince's shoulder, and told him stories of what he had seen in strange lands. He told him of the red ibises, who stand in long rows on the banks of the Nile, and catch gold-fish in their beaks; of the Sphinx, who is as old as

快乐王子

the world itself, and lives in the desert, and knows everything; of the merchants, who walk slowly by the side of their camels, and carry amber beads in their hands; of the King of the Mountains of the Moon, who is as black as ebony, and worships a large crystal; of the great green snake that sleeps in a palm-tree, and has twenty priests to feed it with honey-cakes; and of the pygmies who sail over a big lake on large flat leaves, and are always at war with the butterflies.

"Dear little Swallow," said the Prince, "you tell me of marvellous things, but more marvellous than anything is the suffering of men and of women. There is no Mystery so great as Misery. Fly over my city, little Swallow, and tell me what you see there."

So the Swallow flew over the great city, and saw the rich making merry in their beautiful houses, while the beggars were sitting at the gates. He flew into dark lanes, and saw the white faces of starving children looking out listlessly at the black streets. Under the archway of a bridge two little boys were lying in one another's arms to try and keep themselves warm. "How hungry we are!" they said. "You must not lie here," shouted the Watchman, and they wandered out into the rain.

Then he flew back and told the Prince what he had seen.

"I am covered with fine gold," said the Prince, "you must take it off, leaf by leaf, and give it to my poor; the living always think that gold can make them happy."

Leaf after leaf of the fine gold the Swallow picked off, till the Happy Prince looked quite dull and grey. Leaf after leaf of the fine gold he brought to the poor, and the children's faces grew rosier, and they laughed and played games in the street. "We have bread now!" they cried.

Then the snow came, and after the snow came the frost. The streets looked as if they were made of silver, they were so bright and glistening; long icicles like crystal daggers hung down from the eaves of the houses, everybody went about in furs, and the little boys wore scarlet caps and skated on the ice.

The poor little Swallow grew colder and colder, but he would not leave the Prince, he loved him too well. He picked up crumbs outside the baker's door when the baker was not looking and tried to keep himself warm by flapping his wings.

But at last he knew that he was going to die. He had just strength to fly up to the Prince's shoulder once more. "Good-bye, dear Prince!" he murmured, "will you let me kiss your hand?"

"I am glad that you are going to Egypt at last, little Swallow," said the Prince, "you have stayed too long here; but you must kiss me on the lips, for I love you."

"It is not to Egypt that I am going," said the Swallow. "I am going to the House of Death. Death is the brother of Sleep, is he not?"

And he kissed the Happy Prince on the lips, and fell down dead at his feet.

At that moment a curious crack sounded inside the statue, as if something had broken. The fact is that the leaden heart had snapped right in two. It certainly was a dreadfully hard frost.

Early the next morning the Mayor was walking in the square below in company with the Town Councillors. As they passed the column he looked up at the statue: "Dear me! How shabby the Happy Prince looks!" he said.

"How shabby indeed!" cried the Town Councillors, who always agreed with the Mayor; and they went up to look at it.

"The ruby has fallen out of his sword, his eyes are gone, and he is golden no longer," said the Mayor in fact, "he is litttle better than a beggar!"

"Little better than a beggar," said the Town Councillors.

"And here is actually a dead bird at his feet!" continued the Mayor. "We must really issue a proclamation that birds are not to be allowed to

快
乐
王
子

die here." And the Town Clerk made a note of the suggestion.

So they pulled down the statue of the Happy Prince. "As he is no longer beautiful he is no longer useful," said the Art Professor at the University.

Then they melted the statue in a furnace, and the Mayor held a meeting of the Corporation to decide what was to be done with the metal. "We must have another statue, of course," he said, "and it shall be a statue of myself."

"Of myself," said each of the Town Councillors, and they quarrelled.

"What a strange thing!" said the overseer of the workmen at the foundry. "This broken lead heart will not melt in the furnace. We must throw it away." So they threw it on a dust-heap where the dead Swallow was also lying.

"Bring me the two most precious things in the city," said God to one of His Angels; and the Angel brought Him the leaden heart and the dead bird.

"You have rightly chosen," said God, "for in my garden of Paradise this little bird shall sing for evermore, and in my city of gold the Happy Prince shall praise me."

快
乐
王
子

── 忠实的朋友 ──

一天早晨，老河鼠从自己的洞中探出头来。他长着明亮的小眼睛和硬挺的灰色胡须，尾巴长得像一条长长的黑色橡胶。小鸭子们在池塘里游着水，看上去就像是一大群金丝雀。他们的母亲浑身纯白如雪，再配上一对赤红的腿，正尽力教他们如何头朝下地在水中倒立。

"除非你们学会倒立，否则你们永远不会进入上流社会。"她谆谆告诫，每说一次，就身体力行地演示给小鸭子看。但是小鸭子们并未对她的话引起重视。他们太年轻了，还不知道在上流社会的好处。

"多么顽皮的孩子呀！"老河鼠高声喊道，"他们真该被淹死。"

"不是那么回事，"鸭妈妈回答说，"万事开头难嘛，做父母的要多一点耐心。"

"唉！我完全不了解做父母的情感，"河鼠说，"我是没有成家的人。事实上，我从未结过婚，也不打算结婚。

爱情本身倒是挺好的，但友情比它的价值更高。说实在的，我不知在这世上还有什么比忠实的友谊更崇高和更珍贵。"

"那么，请问，你认为一个忠实的朋友的责任是什么呢？"一只绿色的梅花雀此时正坐在旁边一棵柳树上，听到这段对话后问道。

"是啊，这正是我想知道的。"鸭妈妈说。接着她就游到了池塘的另一头，头朝下倒立起来，为的是给孩子们做一个好榜样。

"这问题问得多笨！"河鼠吼道，"当然，我肯定我忠实的朋友对我是忠实的。"

"那么你又用什么报答呢？"梅花雀说着，跳上了一根银色的枝头，并扑打着他的小翅膀。

"我不明白你的意思。"河鼠回答说。

"那就让我给你讲一个这方面的故事吧。"梅花雀说。

"是关于我的故事吗？"河鼠问道，"如果是的话，我很愿意听，因为我特别喜欢听故事。"

"是与你有关系的。"梅花雀回答说。他飞了下来，站立在河岸边，讲述起那个《忠实的朋友》的故事。

"很久很久以前，"梅花雀说，"有一个诚实的小伙子名叫汉斯。"

"他非常出色吗？"河鼠问道。

"不，"梅花雀答道，"我认为他一点也不出色，只是心肠好罢了，还长着一张滑稽而友善的圆脸。他独自一人住在一间草屋里，每天都在自己的花园里干活。整个乡下没有谁家的花园像他的花园那样可爱。里面长着美国石竹，还有紫罗兰、草荠菜，以及法国的松雪草。有粉红色的玫瑰、金黄色的玫瑰，还有丁香花，紫罗兰有金色的、紫色的和白色的。随着季节的更迭，楼斗菜和酢浆草，马乔莲和野兰香，黄花九轮草和鸢尾草，水仙和丁香都争相开放。一种花刚凋谢，另一种便怒放开来，花园中一直都有美丽的花朵供人观赏，始终都有怡人的芳香可闻。

"小汉斯有许多朋友，但是最忠实的朋友只有磨坊主大休。的确，有钱的磨坊主对小汉斯是非常忠实的，每次他从小汉斯的花园经过，总要从围墙上爬进去摘上一大束鲜花，或者摘上一把香草。硕果累累的季节，他就会往口袋里装满李子和樱桃。

"磨坊主时常对小汉斯说：'真正的朋友应该共享一切。'小汉斯微笑着点点头，他为自己有一位思想如此崇高的朋友而深感骄傲。

"的确，有时候邻居们也感到奇怪，有钱的磨坊主从来没有给过小汉斯任何东西作为回报，尽管他在自己的磨坊里存放了一百袋面粉，还有六头奶牛和一大群绵羊。不过，小汉斯从没有为这些事而苦恼，再说经常听磨坊主对他谈起那些不自私的真正友谊的美妙故事，对小汉

斯来说，没有比听到这些更让他快乐的了。

　　"就这样小汉斯一直在花园中干着活。在春、夏、秋三季中他都很快乐，可冬天一到，他没有水果和鲜花拿到市场上去卖，就要过饥寒交迫的日子，还常常吃不上晚饭，只吃点干梨和核桃就去上床睡觉。在冬天的日子里，他觉得特别孤单，因为这时磨坊主从来不会去看望他。

"磨坊主常常对自己的妻子说：'只要雪没有停，就没有必要去看小汉斯，因为人在困难的时候，就应该让他们独处，不要让外人去打搅他们。这至少是我对友谊的看法，我相信自己是对的，所以我要等到春天到来，那时我会去看望他，他还会送我一大篮樱草，这会使他非常愉快的。'

　　"'你的确为别人想得很周到。'他的妻子答道。她此刻正安坐在舒适的沙发椅上，旁边燃着一大炉柴火，'的确很周到。你谈论起友谊可真有一套，我敢说就是牧师本人也说不出这么美丽的话语，尽管他能住在三层楼的房子里，小手指头上还戴着金戒指。'

　　"'不过我们为什么不请小汉斯来这里呢？'磨坊主的小儿子说，'如果可怜的汉斯遇到困难的话，我会把我的粥分一半给他，还会把我那些小白兔给他看。'

　　"'你真是个傻孩子！'磨坊主大声叫道，'我真不知道送你上学有什么用处。你好像什么也没有学会。噢，假如小汉斯来这里，看见我们暖和的炉火，看见我们丰盛的晚餐，以及大桶的红酒，他可能会妒忌的，而妒忌是一件非常可怕的事情，它会毁了一个人的品性。我当然不愿意把小汉斯的品性给毁了，我是他最要好的朋友，我要一直照顾他，并留心他不受任何诱惑的欺骗。再说，如果小汉斯来到我家，他也许会要我赊点面粉给他，这我可办不到。面粉是一件事，友谊是另一件事，两者不能混为一谈。对呀，这两个词拼写起来差别很大，意思也大不一样。每个人都清楚这一点。'

"'你讲得真好！'磨坊主的妻子说完给自己倒了一大杯温暖的淡啤酒，'我真的感到很困了，就像是坐在教堂里听布道一样。'

"'很多人都做得不错，'磨坊主回答说，'可说得好的人却寥寥无几，可见在两件事中讲话更难一些，也更加迷人一些。'他用严厉的目光望着桌子另一头的小儿子，小儿子感到很不好意思，低下了头，涨红了脸，泪水也忍不住掉进了茶杯中。不过，他年纪这么小，你们还是要原谅他。"

"故事就这么完了吗？"河鼠问。

"当然没有，"梅花雀回答说，"这只是个开头。"

"你太落伍了，"河鼠说，"当今那些故事高手们都是从结尾讲起，然后到开头，最后才讲到中间。这是新方法。这些话是我那天从一位评论家那儿听来的，当时他正同一位年轻人在池塘边散步。对这个问题他作了一番高谈阔论，我相信他是正确的，因为他戴着一副蓝色的眼镜，头也全秃了，而且只要年轻人一开口讲话，他就总回答说'呸！'不过，还是请你把故事讲下去吧。我尤其喜欢那个磨坊主。我自己也有各种美丽的情感，所以我与他是同病相怜。"

"好的，"梅花雀说，他时而用这一只脚跳，时而又用另一只脚跳。"冬天刚一过去，樱草开始开放它们的浅黄色花的时候，磨坊主便对他的妻子说，他准备下山去看望一下小汉斯。

"'啊，你的心肠真好！'他的妻子大声喊道，'你总是想着别人。别忘了带上装花朵的大篮子。'

"于是磨坊主用一根坚实的铁链把风车的翼板固定在一起，随后挎着篮子就下山去了。

"'早上好，小汉斯。'磨坊主说。

"'早上好。'汉斯回答道，他把身体靠在铁铲上，满脸堆着笑容。

"'整个冬天你都过得好吗？'磨坊主又开口问道。

"'啊，是啊，'汉斯大声说，'蒙你相问，你真是太好了，太好了。我要说我过得是有些困难，不过现在春天已经到了，我好快活呀，我的花都长得很好。'

"'今年冬天我们常提起你,'磨坊主说,'不知你过着怎样的日子。'

　　"'太感谢你了,'汉斯说,'我真有点担心你会把我给忘了。'

　　"'汉斯,你说的话让我吃惊,'磨坊主说,'友谊从不会被人忘记,这就是友谊的非凡所在,但是只恐怕你还不懂得生活的诗意。啊,对了,你的樱草长得多可爱呀!'

　　"'它们长得确实可爱,'汉斯说,'我的运气太好了,会有这么多的樱草。我要把它们拿到市场上去,卖给市长的女儿,有了钱就去赎回我的小推车。'

　　"'赎回你的小推车?你的意思是说你卖掉了它?你怎么会干这种事,多么愚蠢啊!'

　　"'噢,事实上,'汉斯说,'我不得不那样做。你知道冬天对我来说是很困难的,我也的确没钱买面包。所以我先是卖掉礼拜日制服上的银纽扣,然后又卖掉银链子,接着卖掉了我的大烟斗,最后才卖掉了我的小推车。不过,我现在要把它们都再买回来。'

　　"'汉斯,'磨坊主说,'我愿意把我的小推车送给你。它还没有完全修好,其实,它有一边已掉了,车轮也有些毛病,但不管怎么说,我还是要把它送给你。我知道我这个人非常慷慨，而且很多人会认为我送你小推车是很愚蠢的举动，但是我是与众不同的人。我认为慷慨是友谊的核心。再说，我还给自己弄了一辆新的小推车。好了，你就放宽心吧，我会把我的小推车给你的。'

"'啊，你太慷慨了，'汉斯说着，那张滑稽有趣的圆脸上洋溢着喜气。'我会毫不费力地把它修好，因为我屋里就有一块木板。'

"'一块木板！'磨坊主说，'对了，我正好想要一块木板来修补我的仓顶。那上面有一个大洞，如果我不堵住它，麦子就会被淋湿。多亏你提到这事，真是好心有好报啊，这真是不可思议。我已经把我的小推车给了你，现在你要把木板给我。其实，小推车比木板要值钱得多，不过真正的友谊从来不会留意这种事的。请快把木板拿来，我今天就动手去修我的仓顶。'

"'当然了，'小汉斯大声说，随即跑进他的小屋，把木板拖了出来。

　　"'这木板不太大，'磨坊主望着木板说，'恐怕等我修完仓顶后就没有剩下来给你修补小推车的了，不过这当然不是我的错。而且现在我已经把我的小推车给了你，我相信你一定乐意给我一些花作回报。给你篮子，注意请给我的篮子装满了。'

　　"'要装满吗？'小汉斯问，脸上显得很不安，因为这可真是一个大篮子，他心里明白，要是把这只篮子装满的话，他就不会有鲜花剩下来拿到集市上去卖了，再说他又非常想把银纽扣赎回来。

　　"'噢，对了，'磨坊主回答说，'既然我已经把自己的小推车给了你，我觉得向你要一些花也算不了什么。也许我是错了，但是我认为友谊，真正的友谊，是不会带有任何私心的。'

　　"'我亲爱的朋友，我最好的朋友，'小汉斯喊了起来，'我这花园里所有的花都供你享用。只要你不怀疑我对你的友谊，至于银纽扣哪一天去赎都可以。'说完他就跑去把花园里所有的美丽樱草都摘了下来，装满了磨坊主的篮子。

忠实的朋友

"'再见了，小汉斯。'磨坊主说。他肩上扛着木板，手里提着大篮子朝山上走去了。

　　"'再见。'小汉斯说，然后他又开始高高兴兴地挖起土来，那辆小推车使他兴奋不已。

　　"第二天，小汉斯正把金盏花藤牵上高高的木架，就听见磨坊主在马路上叫他。他一下子从梯子上跳下来，跑到花园里，朝墙外望去。

　　"只见磨坊主扛着一大袋面粉站在外面。

　　"'亲爱的小汉斯，'磨坊主说，'你愿意帮我把这袋面粉背到集市上去吗？'

　　"'实在对不起，'汉斯说，'我今天真的太忙了。我要把所有的藤蔓一起上架，还得把所有的花浇上水，所有的草都剪平。'

　　"'啊，不错，'磨坊主说，'我想是的。可你要考虑我将把我的小推车送给你，你要是拒绝我就太不够朋友了。'

　　"'啊，不要这么说，'小汉斯大声叫道，'无论如何我也不会对不起朋友的。'他跑进小屋去取帽子，然后扛上那大袋面粉，步履艰难地朝集市走去。

　　"这一天天气炎热，路上尘土飞扬，汉斯还没有走多远，就累得不行了，只好坐下来歇歇脚。不过，他又继续勇敢地上路了，最后终于到达了集市。在那儿他没有等多长时间，就把那袋面粉卖掉了，还卖了个好价钱。他立即动身回家，因为他担心在集市上待得太晚，回去的路上可能会遇上强盗。

"'今天的确太辛苦了，'小汉斯上床睡觉时这样对自己说，'不过我很高兴没有拒绝磨坊主，因为他是我最好的朋友，再说，他还要把他的小推车送给我。'

"第二天一大早，磨坊主就下山来取他那袋面粉的钱，可是小汉斯太累了，这时还躺在床上睡觉呢。

"'我得说，'磨坊主说，'你实在是很懒，想一想我就要把我的小推车送给你，你本该工作得更勤奋才对。懒性是一件大罪，我当然不喜欢我的朋友是个懒汉。你当然不会怪我对你讲了这一番直言，假如我不是你的朋友，我自然也不会这么做的。但是如果人们不能坦诚地说出自己的心里话，那么友谊还有什么意义可言？任何人都可以说漂亮话，可以取悦人，也可以讨好人，然而真正的朋友才总是说逆耳的话，而且不怕给人找苦头吃。的确，真心相交的朋友的确应该如此，因为他知道自己正在做好事。'

"'很对不起，'小汉斯一面说，一面揉着自己的眼睛，脱下了他的睡帽，'不过我真是太累了，我想的只是再睡一小会儿，听听鸟儿的歌声。你知道吗，每当我听过鸟儿的歌声，做起事情总是特别有干劲。'

"'好，这让我很高兴，'磨坊主拍拍小汉斯的肩膀说，'我只想让你穿好衣服立即到我的磨房来，给我修补一下仓顶。'

"可怜的小汉斯当时很想到自己的花园里去干活，因为他的花草已有两天没浇过水了，可他又不想拒绝磨坊主，磨坊主是他的好朋友啊。

"'如果我说我很忙，你会认为我不够朋友吗？'他又害羞又担心地问道。

"'噢，说实在的，'磨坊主回答说，'我觉得我对你的要求并不过分，你想我就要把我的小推车给你，不过当然如果你不想干，我就回去自己动手干。'

"'啊！那怎么行？'小汉斯嚷着说。他从床上跳下来，穿上衣服，往仓房去了。

　　"他在那儿干了整整一天，直到夕阳西下，日落时分磨坊主才来看他干得怎么样了。

　　"'小汉斯，你把仓顶上的洞补好了吗？'磨坊主乐不可支地高声问道。

　　"'全补好了。'小汉斯说着，从梯子上走了下来。

　　"'啊！'磨坊主说，'没有什么比替别人干活更让人快乐的了。'

　　"'听你说话真是莫大的荣幸，'小汉斯坐下身来，一边擦去前额的汗水，一边回答说，'莫大的荣幸，不过我担心我永远也不会有你这么美好的想法。'

　　"'啊！你也会有的，'磨坊主说，'不过你必须得更努力些才行。现在你仅仅完成了友谊的实践，今后有一天你也会具备理论的。'

　　"'你真的这样认为吗？'小汉斯问。

　　"'我对此毫不怀疑，'磨坊主回答说，'不过既然你已经修补好了仓顶，你最好还是回去休息，因为我明天还要你帮我赶山羊到山上去。'

　　"可怜的小汉斯对这件事什么也不敢说，第二天一大早磨坊主就赶着他的羊群来到了小屋旁，汉斯便赶着它们上山去了。他花了整整一天才走了一个来回。回到家时他已经累坏了，就坐在椅子上睡着了，一觉醒来已经是大天亮了。

"'今天能待在自己的花园里我会是多么快乐呀。'说着，他就马上去干活了。

"然而他永远也不能够全身心地去照料好自己的花，因为他的朋友磨坊主老是不停地跑来给他派些差事，或叫他到磨坊去帮忙。有时小汉斯也很苦恼，他担心自己的花会认为他已经把它们给忘了，但是他却用磨坊主是自己最好的朋友这种想法来安慰自己。'再说，'他经常对自己说，'他还要把自己的小推车送给我，那是真正慷慨大方的举动。'

"就这样小汉斯不停地为磨坊主干事，而磨坊主也讲了各种各样关于友谊的美妙语句，汉斯把这些话都记在笔记本上，晚上经常拿出来阅读，因为他还是个爱读书的人。

"有一天晚上，小汉斯正坐在炉旁烤火，忽然传来了响亮的敲门声。这是个气候恶劣的夜晚，风一个劲地在小屋周围狂吹怒吼。起初他还以为听到的只是风声呢，可是又传来了第二次敲门声，接着是第三次，而且比前两次更响亮。

"'这是个可怜的行路人。'小汉斯对自己说，而且朝门口跑去。

"原来门口站着的是磨坊主，他一只手里提着一个马灯，另一只手中拿着一根大拐杖。

"'亲爱的小汉斯，'磨坊主大声叫道，'我遇到大麻烦了。我的小儿子从梯子上掉下来了，受了伤，我准备去请医生。可是医生住的地方太远，今晚的天气又如此恶劣，我刚才突然觉得要是你替我去请医生，会好得多。你知道我将要把我的小推车送给你，所以你应该为我做些事来作为回报，才算是公平的。'

"'当然，'小汉斯大声说道，'我觉得你能来找我是我的荣幸，我这就动身。不过你得把马灯借给我，今晚太黑了，我担心自己跌到水沟里去。'

"'很对不起，'磨坊主回答说，'这可是我的新马灯，如果它出了什么毛病，那对我的损失可就大了。'

"'噢，没关系，我不用它也行。'小汉斯高声说，他取下自己的皮大衣和暖和的红礼帽，又在自己的脖子上围上一条围巾，就动身了。

"那可真是个可怕的风暴之夜，黑得伸手不见五指，小汉斯什么也看不见。风刮得很猛，他连站都站不稳。不过，小汉斯非常勇敢，他走了大约三个钟头，来到了医生的屋前，敲响了门。

　　"'是谁呀？'医生从卧室伸出头来大声问道。

　　"'医生，我是小汉斯。'

　　"'什么事，小汉斯。'

　　"'磨坊主的儿子从梯子上跌下来摔伤了，磨坊主请你马上去。'

　　"'好的！'医生说，并且叫人去备马。他取来大靴子，提上马灯，从楼上走了下来，骑上马朝磨坊主的家奔去，而小汉斯却步履蹒跚地跟在后头。

　　"然而风暴却越来越大，雨下得像小河的流水，小汉斯看不清他面前的路，也赶不上马。最后他迷了路，在一片沼泽地上徘徊着。这是一块非常危险的地方，到处是深深的水坑，可怜的小汉斯就在那里给淹死了。第二天几位牧羊人发现，他的尸体漂浮在一个大池塘的水面上。这几位牧羊人把尸体抬回到他的小屋中。

　　"乡亲们都很喜欢小汉斯，人人都来参加他的葬礼，而磨坊主，则是最主要的哀悼人。"

"'既然我是他最好的朋友，'磨坊主说，'那么就应该让我站最好的位置。'所以他穿一身黑色的长袍走在送葬队伍的最前边，还时不时地用一块大手帕抹着眼泪。

　　"'小汉斯的死的确对每一个人都是个大损失。'铁匠开口说。这时葬礼已经结束，大家都舒适地坐在小酒店里，喝着香酒，吃着甜点。

　　"'无论如何对我是个大损失，'磨坊主回答说，'对了，我都快把我的小推车送给他了，现在我真不知怎么处理它了。放在我家里对我是个大妨碍，它已经破烂不堪，就是卖掉它也值不了什么钱。我今后更要留心不再送人任何东西。大方总让人吃苦头。'"

　　"后来呢？"过了好一会儿河鼠说。

　　"什么，我讲完了。"梅花雀说。

　　"可是磨坊主后来又怎样了呢？"河鼠问道。

　　"噢！我真的不清楚，"梅花雀回答说，"我觉得我不关心这个。"

　　"很显然你的本性中没有同情的成分。"河鼠说。

　　"我恐怕你还没有弄明白这故事中的教义。"梅花雀反驳说。

　　"什么？"河鼠大声叫道。

"教义。"

"你的意思是说这故事里还有一个教义？"

"当然了。"梅花雀说。

"噢，说真的，"河鼠气呼呼地说，"我认为你在讲故事之前就该告诉我那个。如果你那样做了，我肯定不会听你的了。其实，我该像评论家那样说一声'呸！'但是，我现在可以这么说了。"于是他就大喊了一声"呸！"，并挥舞了一下自己的尾巴，回到了山洞中。

"你觉得河鼠怎么样？"鸭妈妈开口问道，她用了好几分钟才拍打着水走上岸来。"他也有好些优点，不过就我而言，我有一个母亲的情怀，只要看见那些铁了心不结婚的单身汉总忍不住要掉下眼泪来。"

"我真担心我把他给得罪了，"梅花雀回答说，"事实是，我给他讲了一个带教义的故事。"

"啊，这事总是很危险的。"鸭妈妈说。

我完全同意她的话。

The Devoted Friend

One morning the old Water-rat put his head out of his hole. He had bright beady eyes and stiff grey whiskers, and his tail was like a long bit of black india-rubber. The little ducks were swimming about in the pond, looking just like a lot of yellow canaries, and their mother, who was pure white with real red legs, was trying to teach them how to stand on their heads in the water.

"You will never be in the best society unless you can stand on your heads," she kept saying to them; and every now and then she showed them how it was done. But the little ducks paid no attention to her. They were so young that they did not know what an advantage it is to be in society at all.

"What disobedient children!" cried the old Water-rat; "they really deserve to be drowned."

"Nothing of the kind,"answered the Duck, "every one must make a beginning, and parents cannot be too patient."

"Ah! I know nothing about the feelings of parents," said the Water-rat; "I am not a family man. In fact, I have never been married, and I never intend to be. Love is all very well in its way, but friendship is much higher. Indeed, I know of nothing in the world that is either nobler or rarer than a devoted friendship."

"And what, pray, is your idea of the duties of a devoted friend?" asked a Green Linnet, who was sitting in a willow-tree hard by, and had overheard the conversation.

"Yes, that is just what I want to know," said the Duck, and she swam away to the end of the pond, and stood upon her head, in order to give her children a good example.

"What a silly question!" cried the Water-rat. "I should expect my devoted friend to be devoted to me, of course."

"And what would you do in return?" said the little bird, swinging upon a silver spray, and flapping his tiny wings.

"I don't understand you," answered the Water-rat.

"Let me tell you a story on the subject," said the Linnet.

夜莺与玫瑰

"Is the story about me?" asked the Water-rat. "If so, I will listen to it, for I am extremely fond of fiction."

"It is applicable to you," answered the Linnet; and he flew down, and alighting upon the bank, he told the story of *The Devoted Friend*.

"Once upon a time," said the Linnet, "there was an honest little fellow named Hans."

"Was he very distinguished?" asked the Water-rat.

"No," answered the Linnet, "I don't think he was distinguished at all, except for his kind heart, and his funny round good-humoured face. He lived in a tiny cottage all by himself, and every day he worked in his garden. In all the countryside there was no garden so lovely as his. Sweet-william grew there, and Gilly-flowers, and Shepherds'-purses, and Fair-maids of France. There were damask Roses, and yellow Roses, lilac Crocuses, and gold, purple Violets and white. Columbine and Lady's-smock, Marjoram and Wild Basil, the Cowslip and the Flower-de-luce, the Daffodil and the Clove-Pink bloomed or blossomed in their proper order as the months went by, one flower taking another flower's place, so that there were always beautiful things to look at, and pleasant odours to smell.

"Little Hans had a great many friends, but the most devoted friend of all was big Hugh the Miller. Indeed, so devoted was the rich Miller to little Hans, that he would never go by his garden without leaning over the wall and plucking a large nosegay, or a handful of sweet herbs, or filling his pockets with plums and cherries if it was the fruit season.

"'Real friends should have everything in common,' the Miller used to say, and little Hans nodded and smiled, and felt very proud of having a friend with such noble ideas.

"Sometimes, indeed, the neighbours thought it strange that the rich Miller never gave little Hans anything in return, though he had a hundred sacks of flour stored away in his mill, and six milk cows, and a large stock of woolly sheep; but Hans never troubled his head about these things, and nothing gave him greater pleasure than to listen to all the wonderful things the Miller used to say about the unselfishness of true friendship.

"So little Hans worked away in his garden. During the spring, the summer, and the autumn he was very happy, but when the winter came, and he had no fruit or flowers to bring to the market, he suffered a good deal from cold and hunger, and often had to go to bed without any supper but a few dried pears or some hard nuts. In the winter, also, he was extremely lonely, as the Miller never came to see him then.

"'There is no good in my going to see little Hans as long as the snow lasts,' the Miller used to say to his wife, 'for when people are in trouble they should be left alone, and not be bothered by visitors. That at least is my idea about friendship, and I am sure I am right. So I shall wait till the spring comes, and then I shall pay him a visit, and he will be able to give me a large basket of primroses, and that will make him so happy.'

"'You are certainly very thoughtful about others,'

忠
实
的
朋
友

answered the Wife, as she sat in her comfortable armchair by the big pinewood fire; 'very thoughtful indeed. It is quite a treat to hear you talk about friendship. I am sure the clergyman himself could not say such beautiful things as you do, though he does live in a three-storied house, and wears a gold ring on his little finger.'

"'But could we not ask little Hans up here?' said the Miller's youngest son. 'If poor Hans is in trouble I will give him half my porridge, and show him my white rabbits.'

"'What a silly boy you are!' cried the Miller; 'I really don't know what is the use of sending you to school. You seem not to learn anything. Why, if little Hans came up here, and saw our warm fire, and our good supper, and our great cask of red wine, he might get envious, and envy is a most terrible thing, and would spoil anybody's nature. I certainly will not allow Hans's nature to be spoiled. I am his best friend, and I will always watch over him, and see that he is not led into any temptations. Besides, if Hans came here, he might ask me to let him have some flour on credit, and that I could not do. Flour is one thing, and friendship is another, and they should not be confused. Why, the words are spelt differently, and mean quite different things. Everybody can see that.'

"'How well you talk!' said the Miller's Wife, pouring herself out a large glass of warm ale; 'really I feel quite drowsy. It is just like being in church.'

"'Lots of people act well,' answered the Miller; 'but very few people talk well, which shows that talking is much the more difficult thing of the two, and much the finer thing also;' and he looked sternly across the table at his little son, who felt so ashamed of himself that he hung his head down, and grew quite scarlet, and began to cry into his tea. However, he was so young that you must excuse him."

"Is that the end of the story?" asked the Water-rat.

"Certainly not," answered the Linnet, "that is the beginning."

"Then you are quite behind the age," said the

Water-rat. "Every good story-teller nowadays starts with the end, and then goes on to the beginning, and concludes with the middle. That is the new method. I heard all about it the other day from a critic who was walking round the pond with a young man. He spoke of the matter at great length, and I am sure he must have been right, for he had blue spectacles and a bald head, and whenever the young man made any remark, he always answered 'Pooh!' But pray go on with your story. I like the Miller immensely. I have all kinds of beautiful sentiments myself, so there is a great sympathy between us."

"Well," said the Linnet, hopping now on one leg and now on the other, "as soon as the winter was over, and the primroses began to open their pale yellow stars, the Miller said to his wife that he would go down and see little Hans.

"'Why, what a good heart you have!' cried his wife; 'you are always thinking of others. And mind you take the big basket with you for the flowers.'

"So the Miller tied the sails of the windmill together with a strong iron chain, and went down the hill with the basket on his arm.

"'Good morning, little Hans,' said the Miller.

"'Good morning,' said Hans, leaning on his spade, and smiling from ear to ear.

"'And how have you been all the winter?' said the Miller.

"'Well, really,' cried Hans, 'it is very good of you to ask, very good indeed. I am afraid I had rather a hard time of it, but now the spring has come, and I am quite happy, and all my flowers are doing well.'

"'We often talked of you during the winter, Hans,'said the Miller, 'and wondered how you were getting on.'

"'That was kind of you,' said Hans; 'I was half afraid you had forgotten me.'

"'Hans, I am surprised at you,' said the Miller; 'friendship never forgets. That is the wonderful thing about it, but I am afraid you don't understand the poetry of life. How lovely your primroses are looking, by-the-by!'

"'They are certainly very lovely,' said Hans, 'and it is a most lucky thing for me that I have so many. I am going to bring them into the market and sell them to the Burgomaster's daughter, and buy back my wheelbarrow with the money.'

"'Buy back your wheelbarrow? You don't mean to say you have sold it? What a very stupid thing to do!'

"'Well, the fact is,' said Hans, 'that I was obliged to. You see the winter was a very bad time for me, and I really had no money at all to buy bread with. So I first sold the silver buttons off my Sunday coat, and then I sold my silver chain, and then I sold my big pipe, and at last I sold my wheelbarrow. But I am going to buy them all back again now.'

"'Hans,' said the Miller, 'I will give you my wheelbarrow. It is not in very good repair; indeed, one side is gone, and there is something wrong with the wheel-spokes; but in spite of that I will give it to you. I know it is very generous of me, and a great many people would think me extremely foolish for parting with it, but I am not like the rest of the world. I think that generosity is the essence of friendship, and, besides, I have got a new wheelbarrow for myself. Yes, you may set your mind at ease, I will give you my wheelbarrow.'

"'Well, really, that is generous of you,' said little Hans, and his funny round face glowed all over with pleasure. 'I can easily put it in repair, as I have a plank of wood in the house.'

"'A plank of wood!' said the Miller; 'why, that is just what I want for the roof of my barn. There is a very large hole in it, and the corn will all get damp if I don't stop it up. How lucky you mentioned it! It is quite remarkable how one good action always breeds another. I have given you my wheelbarrow, and now you are going to give me your plank. Of course, the wheelbarrow is worth far more than the plank, but true friendship never notices things like that. Pray get it at once, and I will set to work at my barn this very day.'

"'Certainly,' cried little Hans, and he ran into the

shed and dragged the plank out.

"'It is not a very big plank,' said the Miller, looking at it, 'and I am afraid that after I have mended my barn-roof there won't be any left for you to mend the wheelbarrow with; but, of course, that is not my fault. And now, as I have given you my wheelbarrow, I am sure you would like to give me some flowers in return. Here is the basket, and mind you fill it quite full.'

"'Quite full?' said little Hans, rather sorrowfully, for it was really a very big basket, and he knew that if he filled it he would have no flowers left for the market, and he was very anxious to get his silver buttons back.

"'Well, really,'answered the Miller,'as I have given you my wheelbarrow, I don't think that it is much to ask you for a few flowers. I may be wrong, but I should have thought that friendship, true friendship, was quite free from selfishness of any kind.'

"'My dear friend, my best friend,'cried little Hans, 'you are welcome to all the flowers in my garden. I would much sooner have your good opinion than my silver buttons, any day;' and he ran and plucked all his pretty primroses, and filled the Miller's basket.

"'Good-bye, little Hans,'said the Miller, as he went up the hill with the plank on his shoulder, and the big basket in his hand.

"'Good-bye,'said little Hans, and he began to dig away quite merrily, he was so pleased about the wheelbarrow.

"The next day he was nailing up some honeysuckle against the porch, when he heard the Miller's voice calling to him from the road. So he jumped off the ladder, and ran down the garden, and looked over the wall.

"There was the Miller with a large sack of flour on his back.

"'Dear little Hans,'said the Miller,'would you mind carrying this sack of flour for me to market?'

"'Oh, I am so sorry,' said Hans,'but I am really very busy today. I have got all my creepers to nail up, and all my flowers to water, and all my grass to roll.'

"'Well, really,' said the Miller, 'I think that,

忠实的朋友

considering that I am going to give you my wheelbarrow, it is rather unfriendly of you to refuse.'

"'Oh, don't say that,' cried little Hans, 'I wouldn't be unfriendly for the whole world;' and he ran in for his cap, and trudged off with the big sack on his shoulders.

"It was a very hot day, and the road was terribly dusty, and before Hans had reached the sixth milestone he was so tired that he had to sit down and rest. However, he went on bravely, and at last he reached the market. After he had waited there some time, he sold the sack of flour for a very good price, and then he returned home at once, for he was afraid that if he stopped too late he might meet some robbers on the way.

"'It has certainly been a hard day,' said little Hans to himself as he was going to bed, 'but I am glad I did not refuse the Miller, for he is my best friend, and, besides, he is going to give me his wheelbarrow.'

"Early the next morning the Miller came down to get the money for his sack of flour, but little Hans was so tired that he was still in bed.

"'Upon my word,'said the Miller, 'you are very lazy. Really, considering that I am going to give you my wheelbarrow, I think you might work harder. Idleness is a great sin, and I certainly don't like any of my friends to be idle or sluggish. You must not mind my speaking quite plainly to you. Of course I should not dream of doing so if I were not your friend. But what is the good of friendship if one cannot say exactly what one means? Anybody can say charming things and try to please and to flatter, but a true friend always says unpleasant things, and does not mind giving pain. Indeed, if he is a really true friend he prefers it, for he knows that then he is doing good.'

"'I am very sorry,' said little Hans, rubbing his eyes and pulling off his night-cap, 'but I was so tired that I thought I would lie in bed for a little time, and listen to the birds singing. Do you know that I always work better after hearing the birds sing?'

"'Well, I am glad of that,' said the Miller, clapping little Hans on the back,'for I want you to come up to the

忠
实
的
朋
友

103

mill as soon as you are dressed, and mend my barn-
roof for me.'

"Poor little Hans was very anxious to go and work
in his garden, for his flowers had not been watered for
two days, but he did not like to refuse the Miller, as he
was such a good friend to him.

"'Do you think it would be unfriendly of me if I said I
was busy?' he inquired in a shy and timid voice.

"'Well, really,' answered the Miller, 'I do not think
it is much to ask of you, considering that I am going to
give you my wheelbarrow; but of course if you refuse I
will go and do it myself.'

"'Oh! On no account,' cried little Hans and he
jumped out of bed, and dressed himself, and went up
to the barn.

"He worked there all day long, till sunset, and at
sunset the Miller came to see how he was getting on.

"'Have you mended the hole in the roof yet, little
Hans?' cried the Miller in a cheery voice.

"'It is quite mended,' answered little Hans, coming

down the ladder.

"'Ah!' said the Miller, 'there is no work so delightful as the work one does for others.'

"'It is certainly a great privilege to hear you talk,' answered little Hans, sitting down and wiping his forehead, 'a very great privilege. But I am afraid I shall never have such beautiful ideas as you have.'

"'Oh! They will come to you,' said the Miller, 'but you must take more pains. At present you have only the practice of friendship; some day you will have the theory also.'

"'Do you really think I shall?' asked little Hans.

"'I have no doubt of it,' answered the Miller; 'but now that you have mended the roof, you had better go home and rest, for I want you to drive my sheep to the mountain to-morrow."

"Poor little Hans was afraid to say anything to this, and early the next morning the Miller brought his sheep round to the cottage, and Hans started off with them to the mountain. It took him the whole day to get there

忠实的朋友

and back; and when he returned he was so tired that he went off to sleep in his chair, and did not wake up till it was broad daylight.

"'What a delightful time I shall have in my garden,'he said, and he went to work at once.

"But somehow he was never able to look after his flowers at all, for his friend the Miller was always coming round and sending him off on long errands, or getting him to help at the mill. Little Hans was very much distressed at times, as he was afraid his flowers would think he had forgotten them, but he consoled himself by the reflection that the Miller was his best friend. 'Besides,'he used to say, 'he is going to give me his wheelbarrow, and that is an act of pure generosity.'

"So little Hans worked away for the Miller, and the Miller said all kinds of beautiful things about friendship, which Hans took down in a note-book, and used to read over at night, for he was a very good scholar.

"Now it happened that one evening little Hans was sitting by his fireside when a loud rap came at the door.

夜
莺
与
玫
瑰

It was a very wild night, and the wind was blowing and roaring round the house so terribly that at first he thought it was merely the storm. But a second rap came, and then a third, louder than either of the others.

"'It is some poor traveller,' said little Hans to himself, and he ran to the door.

"There stood the Miller with a lantern in one hand and a big stick in the other.

"'Dear little Hans,' cried the Miller, 'I am in great trouble. My little boy has fallen off a ladder and hurt himself, and I am going for the Doctor. But he lives so far away, and it is such a bad night, that it has just occurred to me that it would be much better if you went instead of me. You know I am going to give you my wheelbarrow, and so, it is only fair that you should do something for me in return.'

"'Certainly,' cried little Hans, 'I take it quite as a compliment your coming to me, and I will start off at once. But you must lend me your lantern, as the night is so dark that I am afraid I might fall into the ditch.'

"'I am very sorry,' answered the Miller, 'but it is my new lantern, and it would be a great loss to me if anything happened to it.'

"'Well, never mind, I will do without it,' cried little Hans, and he took down his great fur coat, and his warm scarlet cap, and tied a muffler round his throat, and started off.

"What a dreadful storm it was! The night was so black that little Hans could hardly see, and the wind was so strong that he could scarcely stand. However, he was very courageous, and after he had been walking about three hours, he arrived at the Doctor's house, and knocked at the door.

"'Who is there?' cried the Doctor, putting his head out of his bedroom window.

"'Little Hans, Doctor.'

"'What do you want, little Hans?'

"'The Miller's son has fallen from a ladder, and has hurt himself, and the Miller wants you to come at once.'

"'All right!' said the Doctor; and he ordered his

horse, and his big boots, and his lantern, and came downstairs, and rode off in the direction of the Miller's house, little Hans trudging behind him.

"But the storm grew worse and worse, and the rain fell in torrents, and little Hans could not see where he was going, or keep up with the horse. At last he lost his way, and wandered off on the moor, which was a very dangerous place, as it was full of deep holes, and there poor little Hans was drowned. His body was found the next day by some goatherds, floating in a great pool of water, and was brought back by them to the cottage.

"Everybody went to little Hans's funeral, as he was so popular, and the Miller was the chief mourner.

"'As I was his best friend,' said the Miller, 'it is only fair that I should have the best place;' so he walked at the head of the procession in a long black cloak, and every now and then he wiped his eyes with a big pocket-handkerchief.

"'Little Hans is certainly a great loss to every one,'said the Blacksmith, when the funeral was over, and they were all seated comfortably in the inn, drinking spiced wine and eating sweet cakes.

"'A great loss to me at any rate,' answered the Miller; 'why, I had as good as given him my wheelbarrow, and now I really don't know what to do with it. It is very much in my way at home, and it is in such bad repair that I could not get anything for it if I sold it. I will certainly take care not to give away anything again. One always suffers for being generous.'"

"Well?" said the Water-rat, after a long pause.

"Well, that is the end," said the Linnet.

"But what became of the Miller?" asked the Water-rat.

"Oh! I really don't know," replied the Linnet, "and I am sure that I don't care."

"It is quite evident then that you have no sympathy in your nature," said the Water-rat.

"I am afraid you don't quite see the moral of the story," remarked the Linnet.

"The what?" screamed the Water-rat.

"The moral."

"Do you mean to say that the story has a moral?"

"Certainly," said the Linnet.

"Well, really," said the Water-rat, in a very angry manner, "I think you should have told me that before you began. If you had done so, I certainly would not have listened to you; in fact, I should have said 'Pooh,' like the critic. However, I can say it now;" so he shouted out "Pooh" at the top of his voice, gave a whisk with his tail, and went back into his hole.

"And how do you like the Water-rat?" asked the Duck, who came paddling up some minutes afterwards. "He has a great many good points, but for my own part I have a mother's feelings, and I can never look at a confirmed bachelor without the tears coming into my eyes."

"I am rather afraid that I have annoyed him," answered the Linnet. "The fact is, that I told him a story with a moral."

"Ah! That is always a very dangerous thing to do," said the Duck.

And I quite agree with her.

忠
实
的
朋
友

了不起的火箭

王子就要结婚了，人人都露出欢欣的神情。他已经等了新娘整整一年，如今她终于来了。她是一位俄国公主，坐着由六只驯鹿拉的雪橇从芬兰一路赶来。雪橇看上去像一只巨大的金色天鹅，小公主就安卧在天鹅的两只翅膀之间。那件长长的貂皮大衣一直垂到她的脚跟，她的头上戴着一顶小巧的银线帽子，她的肤色苍白得就如同她一直居住的雪宫的颜色。她是如此苍白，在她驶过街道的时候，沿街的人们都惊讶地叹道："她就像一朵白玫瑰！"于是大家纷纷从阳台上朝她抛下鲜花。

在城堡的门口，王子正等着迎接她的到来。他有一双梦幻般的紫色眼睛和一头金黄色的头发。一看见她来了，他就单膝跪下，吻了她的手。

"你的照片好漂亮，"他轻声地说，"不过你比照片更漂亮。"小公主的脸一下子就红了。

"她先前像一朵白玫瑰，"一位年轻的侍卫对身边的

人说，"可此刻却像一朵红玫瑰了。"整个宫里的人都快乐无比。

这以后的三天中人人都说着："白玫瑰，红玫瑰；红玫瑰，白玫瑰。"于是国王下令给那个侍卫的薪金增加一倍。不过他根本就没有薪水，因此奖励对他来说还是一无所有，然而这被视为一种莫大的荣誉，并按惯例在宫廷报纸上登出。

三天过后便举行了婚礼庆典。这是一次盛大的仪式，新郎和新娘手牵着手，走在一幅绣着小珍珠的紫色鹅绒华盖下。接着又举行了国宴，持续了五小时。王子和公主坐在大厅的首座上，用一只清亮的水晶杯子饮酒。只有真正相爱的人才能用这只杯子喝酒，因为只要虚伪的嘴唇一挨上杯子，杯子就会变得灰暗无光。

了不起的火箭

"一眼就能看出他们相亲相爱，"那个小侍卫说，"如同水晶一样纯洁！"为这句话国王再次下令给他加薪。"多么大的荣耀啊！"群臣们异口同声地喊道。

宴会之后举办了舞会，新郎和新娘将要一块儿跳舞，国王答应为他们吹笛子。他吹得很难听，可没有人敢对他那么说，因为他是一国之君。说真的，他只会吹两种调子，并且从来也没有人搞清楚他吹的是哪一种，不过也无关紧要，因为不管他吹的是什么，人们都会高喊狂叫："棒极了！棒极了！"

最后一个节目是放盛大的烟花，燃放的时间定在午夜。小公主从来没有看过放烟花，因此国王下令皇家烟花手要亲自出席当天的婚礼以便放烟花。

"烟花是什么样子？"有一天早上，小公主在露天阳台上散步时这样问王子。

"它们就像北极光，"国王说，他一贯喜欢替别人回答问题，"只是更自然罢了。我本人更喜欢烟花而不是星星，因为你一直都明白它们何时会出现，它们就如同我吹笛子一样美妙。你一定要看看它们。"

就这样，在御花园的尽头搭起了一座大台子。等皇家烟花手把一切都准备完毕，烟花们便相互交谈起来。

"世界真是太美丽了，"一个小鞭炮大声喊道，"看看那些黄色的郁金香。啊！如果它们是真正的鞭炮，它们会更逗人喜爱的。我很高兴我经常旅游。旅游大大增长见识，并能打消一切个人的偏见。"

"国王的花园不是世界，你这个傻鞭炮，"一枚罗马烛光烟花说，"世界是一个大得很的地方，你要花三天时间才能看遍全世界。"

"任何地方只要你爱它，它就是你的世界，"一枚深思熟虑的旋转烟花伤感地说。她早年曾恋上一只旧的杉木箱子，并以这段伤心的经历而自豪。"不过爱情已不再时髦了，诗人们把它给扼杀了。他们对爱情抒发得太多，使人们不再相信爱情了。对此，我一点也不觉得吃惊。真正的爱情是痛苦的、是沉默的。我记得自己曾有过那么一回——可是现在已经结束了。浪漫只属于过去。"

"胡说！"罗马烛光烟花说，"浪漫永远不会消亡，它犹如月亮一样，永远活着。比如，这对新婚夫妇，他俩就非常相亲相爱，关于他们的故事我是今天早晨从一枚棕色纸做的礼花弹那儿听来的，他碰巧跟我同在一个抽屉里面，并且知道最新的宫中消息。"

可是，只见旋转烟花摇摇头，喃喃地说："浪漫已经消亡了，浪漫已经消亡了，已经消亡了。"她和其他许多人一样，相信假如你把同一件事情反复说上许多次，最后假的也会变成真的。

突然，传来一声尖尖的干咳声，他们都转头四下张望。

这声音来自一个高大的，模样傲慢的火箭，它被绑在一根长木棍的顶端。它在发表言论之前，总要先咳上几声，好引起人们的注意。

"啊咳！啊咳！"他咳嗽着。大家都认真地听着，只有可怜的旋转烟花仍旧摇着头，喃喃地说："浪漫已经消亡了。"

"肃静！肃静！"一只爆竹大声嚷道。他是个政客似的人物，在本地的选举中总能独占鳌头，因此他深知如何使用恰当的政治术语。

"死光了。"旋转烟花低语道，说完她就去睡觉了。

等到周围完全安静下来时，火箭发出第三次咳嗽声，并开始了发言。他的语调既缓慢又清晰，好像是在背诵什么东西，对他的听众他从来不正眼去看。说实在的，他的风度是非常出众的。

"王子真是幸运啊，"他说道，"他结婚的日子正好是

夜莺与玫瑰

118

我要升天燃放的时候。真是的，就算是事先安排好的，对他来说也没有比这更好的了；但话又说回来，王子们总是交好运的。"

"我的妈呀！"小鞭炮说，"我的想法却正好相反，我想我们是托王子的福才得以升天燃放的。"

"对于你来说可能是这样的，"他回答说，"事实上这一点是肯定无疑的。不过对我而言事情就不一样了。我是一枚了不起的火箭，出身于一个了不起的家庭。我母亲是她那个时代最出名的旋转烟花，并以她优美的舞姿而著称。只要她一出场亮相，她要旋转十九次才会飞出去，每转上一次，她就会向空中抛撒七颗粉红的彩星。她的直径有三英尺 ❶ 半，是用最好的火药制成的。我的父亲像我一样也是火箭，他有法国血统。他飞得可真高，人们都担心他不会下来了。尽管如此，他还是下来了，因为他性格善良。他化作一阵金色的雨，非常耀眼地落了下来。报纸用足吹捧的词句描述他的表演。的确，宫廷的报纸把他称为烟花 ❷ 艺术的一个伟大成就。"

---

❶ 1英尺约为0.3米。

❷ 火箭错将pyrotechnic（烟花的）中的"r"读成了"l"，此处讽刺了火箭的傲慢、无知。

"烟花,烟花,你是指它吗?"一枚孟加拉烟花说,"我知道它是烟花,因为我看见我的匣子上写着呢。"

"噢,我说的是烟花。"火箭语调严肃地回答说。孟加拉烟花感到自己受到极大的凌辱,于是立即去欺负那些小鞭炮了,为了表明自己依旧是个重要的角色。

"我是说,"火箭继续说,"我是说——我说的是什么?"

"你在说你自己。"罗马烛光烟花回答说。

"的确,我知道我正在讨论某个有趣的话题,却被人给粗暴地打断了。我讨厌各种粗鲁的举止和不良行为,因为我是个非常敏感的人。全世界没有哪个人比我更敏感了,对此我深信不疑。"

"一个敏感的人是指什么?"鞭炮问罗马烛光烟花。

"一个人因为自己脚上生鸡眼,便总想着踩别人的脚趾头。"罗马烛光烟花低声耳语道。鞭炮差一点没笑破肚皮。

"喂,你笑什么呀?"火箭开口问道,"我都没笑。"

"我笑是因为我高兴。"鞭炮回答说。

"这理由太自私了,"火箭脸带怒色地说,"你有什么权利高兴?你应该为别人想想。实际上,你应该为我想想。我总是想着我自己,我也希望别人都会这么做。这就是所谓的同情。这是个可爱的美德,我这方面的德性就很高。例如，假定今天夜里我出了什么事，那么对每一个人来说会是多么不幸！王子和公主再也不会开心了，他们的婚后生活将会被毁掉；至于国王，他或许经不住这场打击。真的，我一想起自己所处的重要地位，我几乎感动得流下眼泪。"

"如果你想给别人带来快乐，"罗马烛光烟花说，"那么你最好先不要把自己弄得湿乎乎的。"

"当然了，"孟加拉烟花说，他现在的精神好多了，"这是个简单的常识。"

"常识，一点不假！"火箭愤愤不平地说，"可你忘了我是很了不起的，而且非常了不起。啊，任何人如若没有想象力的话，也会具备常识的。然而我有想象力，因为我从没有把事物按照它们实际的情况去考虑，我总是把它们想象成另外一回事。至于要我本人不要流泪，很显然在场的各位没人能够欣赏多愁善感的品性。所幸的是我本人并不介意。能够让我维持一生的唯一事就是想到自己要比别人优越得多。这也是我一贯培养的感觉。你们这些人都是没有情感的。你们只会傻笑或开玩笑，好像王子和公主不是刚刚结婚似的。"

"啊，正是，"一枚小火球动情地叫道，"难道不行吗？

这是一件多大的喜事呀，我只要一飞到天上去，我就会把这一切都讲给星星听。等我给它们讲起美丽的公主，你会看见星星们在眨眼睛。"

"啊！多么浅薄的人生观！"火箭说，"然而这正是我所预料的。你们胸无大志；你们既浅薄又无知。噢，或许王子和公主会到有条深深河流的乡村去住；或许他们只有一个儿子，那个小男孩像王子一样有一头金发和紫色眼睛；或许有一天小男孩会跟保姆一起出去散步；或许保姆会在一棵大树下睡觉；或许小男孩会掉进深深的流水中淹死。多么可怕的灾难啊！可怜的人儿，失去了他们唯一的儿子！这真是太可怕了！我永远也忘不了。"

"但是他们并没有失去他们的独子呀，"罗马烛光烟花说，"根本就没有任何不幸发生在他们身上。"

"我从没说过他们会发生不幸，"火箭回答说，"我只是说他们可能会。如果他们已经失去了独生子，那么再谈此事还有什么意思？我讨厌那些马后炮的人。不过一想到他们可能会失去独子，我就会非常难过。"

"你当然会的！"孟加拉烟花大声嚷道，"实际上，你是我所遇到的最感情用事的人。"

"你是我所遇到的最粗俗的人，"火箭反驳说，"你是无法理解我对王子的友情的。"

"得了，你甚至还不认识他呢。"罗马烛光烟花怒吼道。

"我从未说过我认识他。"火箭回答说，"我敢说，如果我认识他，我是不会成为他的朋友的。认识好多朋友，是件非常危险的事。"

"说真的你最好还是不要流眼泪，"火球说，"这可是件要紧的事。"

"我敢肯定，对你是非常要紧，"火箭回答说，"可我想哭就得哭。"说着他还真的哭了起来，泪水像雨点一样从木棍上流下来，差一点淹死两只正在寻找一块干燥的好地方做窝的小甲虫。

"他必定有真正的浪漫品质，"旋转烟花说，"根本就没有什么可哭的，他却能哭得起来。"接着她长叹一口气，又想起了那个杉木箱子。

不过罗马烛光烟花和孟加拉烟花却是老大不乐意，他们不停地说着："胡扯！胡扯！"那声音可真够大的。他们是非常讲实际的，只要是他们反对的东西，他们就会说是胡扯。

这时明月像一面银色的盾牌冉冉升起；繁星开始闪烁，音乐声从宫中传来。

王子和公主正在领舞。他们跳得可真美，就连那些亭亭玉立的白莲花也透过窗户偷看他俩，大朵的红色罂粟花频频点头，并打着节拍。

随后十点的钟声敲响了，接着十一点的钟声敲响了，然后是十二点。当午夜最后一下钟声敲响时，所有的人都来到了露天阳台上，国王派人去叫皇家烟花手。

"开始放烟花吧。"国王宣布说。皇家烟花手深深地鞠了一躬，并迈步向下走到花园的尽头。他带了六个助手，每个助手都拿着一根竿子，竿子的顶头捆着一个点燃的火把。

这的确是一场空前盛大的表演。

飕飕！飕飕！旋转烟花飞了上去，一边飞一边旋转着。轰隆！轰隆！罗马烛光烟花又飞了上去。然后爆竹们便到处狂舞起来，接着孟加拉烟花把一切都映成了红彤彤的。"再见了！"火球喊了一声就腾空而去，抛下无数蓝色的小火星。啪啪！啦啦！大爆竹们也跟着响了，他们真是痛快无比。他们个个都非常成功，只剩下了不起的火箭了。他浑身哭得湿乎乎的，根本就无法升空上天。他身上最好的东西只有火药，火药被泪水打湿后，就什么用场也派不上了。他的那些穷亲戚们，平时他从未打过招呼，只是偶尔讥讽一下，此刻个个都像盛开着的燃烧的金色花朵，飞到天空中去了。好哇！好哇！宫廷的人们都欢呼起来；小公主高兴得笑个不停。

"我猜想他们留着我是为了某个更盛大的庆典，"火箭说，"毫无疑问就是这个意思。"他看上去比以前还要傲慢。

第二天工人们来清理园子。"这些人一看就是代表团，"火箭说，"我要摆点架子才好。"于是他就摆出一副威严的样子，庄重地皱着眉头，仿佛在思考什么重要的问题似的。可是工人们一点也没有理睬他，直到要离开的时候，他们中的一人碰巧看见了他。"嘿！"他大喊了一声，"这么破的一枚火箭！"说完他便把火箭丢到墙外的阴沟里去了。

"破火箭？破火箭？"他在空中一边翻滚着一边说，"不可能！大火箭，那个人就是这么说的。'破'和'大'这两个发音是非常接近的，的确它们常常是一样的发音。"接着他就掉进了阴沟里。

"这里并不舒服，"他说，"可没准是个时髦的浴场，他们是送我来休养的。我的精神的确受到极大的伤害，我也需要休息了。"

这时一只小青蛙朝他游了过来，他有一双明亮闪光的宝石眼睛，和一件绿色斑纹的外衣。

"看来，是位新来的客人！"青蛙说，"毕竟，任谁也不会喜欢污泥的，下点雨，有个池塘，我便会十分幸福。你认为下午会下雨吗？我真希望如此，可你看这蓝蓝的天空，万里无云，多么可惜啊！"

"啊咳！啊咳！"火箭说着便咳了起来。

"你的声音多好听啊！"青蛙大声叫道，"真像是青蛙的呱呱叫声，这种呱呱声当然是世界上最美妙的音乐了。今天晚上你可以来听听我们合唱队的演出。我们都在农夫房屋旁的池塘中，月亮一升起我们便开始表演。那可太迷人了，人人都睁着双眼躺着听我们唱。其实，就在昨天我还听农夫的妻子对她的母亲说，就是因为我们的存在，她整夜一点儿也睡不着。能受到这么多人的欢迎，真是谢天谢地。"

"啊咳！啊咳！"火箭生气地说。由于连一句话也插不进去，他感到非常恼火。

"当然了，美妙的音乐，"青蛙继续说，"我希望你能到鸭池来。我要去看我的女儿们了。我有六个漂亮的女儿，我很担心她们会遇到梭鱼。他是个十足的恶魔，会毫不

犹豫地拿她们当早餐吃掉。好了，再见，我们的谈话真
让我开心，我信得过你。"

　　"这是谈话吗？"火箭说，"都是你一个人在说话，
那不算谈话。"

　　"总得要人听啊，"青蛙回答说，"我也喜欢自言自语。
这节省时间，且避免争吵。"

　　"可我喜欢争吵。"火箭说。

　　"我不希望这样，"青蛙得意地说，"争吵太粗俗了，
因为在好的社会中，人人都会持有完全一致的意见。再
一次告别了，我看见我的女儿在那边。"说完小青蛙就游
走了。

　　"你是个非常讨厌的家伙，"火箭说，"而且教养很
差。我讨厌人们只顾谈论自己，就像你这样，要知道此
时别人也想说说话，就像我这样。这就是我所说的自私，
自私是十分可恶的事，特别是对于我这种品性的人来说，

因为我是以同情心而出了名的。说实在的，你应该以我为学习榜样，你或许找不到比我更好的榜样了。既然你还有机会，你最好把握住，因为我差不多马上就要返回宫中去了。我在宫中是个大宠儿；其实，王子和公主在昨天就为庆祝我而举办了婚礼。当然，这些事你是一无所知的，因为你是个乡巴佬。"

"跟他讲话没有用处，"一只蜻蜓开口说，他此刻正坐在一株棕色的香蒲顶上，"是没有用处的，因为他已经走开了。"

"嗯，那是他的损失，不是我的，"火箭回答说。"我不会仅仅因为他不理会我，就停止对他说话。我喜欢听自己讲话，这是我最大的乐趣之一。我常常一个人讲上一大堆话，我太聪明了，有时候我连我自己讲的话也不懂。"

"那么你真应该去讲授哲学。"蜻蜓说完，展开自己一对可爱的纱翼朝空中飞去了。

"他不留在这儿，真是傻极了！"火箭说，"我敢说他并不是经常有这样的机会来提高智力的。然而，我一点也不介意。像我这样的天才肯定有一天会得人赏识的。"他往稀泥中陷得更深了。

过了一会儿一只白色的大鸭子向他游了过来。她有一对黄色的腿和一双蹼。她走起路来风韵十足，人们都叫她大美人。

"嘎，嘎，嘎，"她叫着说，"你的样子多么古怪啊！你生下来就长这样吗？或者是一次事故造成的？"

"很显然，你一直都住在乡下，"火箭回答说，"不然你会知道我是谁的。不过，我会原谅你的无知。期望别人跟自己一样了不起是不公平的。等你听说我能够飞上天空并撒下一阵金色的雨点后，你一定会感到惊讶的。"

"我倒不看重那个，"鸭子说，"因为我看不出它对别人会有什么好处。眼下，要是你能像牛一样地去犁地，像马一样地去拉车，或像牧羊犬那样地照看羊群，那还算是个人物。"

"我的朋友啊，"火箭用十分高傲的语气大声说道，"可见你是属于下等阶层的。我这样身份的人是从来不讲什么用处的。我们有某些特别的才能，那就足够了。我本人对各种所谓的勤劳并没有好感，尤其对像你赞赏的那些勤劳更是一点好感也没有。说实话，我一贯认为做艰苦的工作仅仅是那些无事可干的人们的一种逃避方式。"

"好吧，好吧，"鸭子说，她是个处事平稳的人，也从未跟任何人争吵过，"各人有各人的爱好。我想，无论如何，你要在这儿安家落户了吧。"

"啊！当然不会了，"火箭嚷道，"我只是个过路人，一位有名望的客人。事实是我觉得这地方好无聊。这儿既不宁静，又没有社交生活。说实在的，这儿根本就是郊外。我可能要回到宫里去，因为我注定了要在世界上做一番成就的。"

"我也曾想过要投身于公众事业中去，"鸭子说，"世上有那么多需要革新的事物。老实说，我前不久干过一阵会议主席的工作，我们通过决议谴责一切我们不喜欢的东西。然而，那些决议好像并没有多大效果。现在我一心从事家务，照顾我的家庭。"

"我生来就是为了干大事的，"火箭说，"我所有的亲戚也都是如此，甚至包括他们中最卑微的。只要我们一出场，随时都会引起广泛的关注。其实还没轮到我出场呢，不过只要我一出现，准会是壮观的场面。说到家务事，它会使人早早地衰老，并无心追求更高的目标。"

"啊！更高的目标，它们该有多好呀！"鸭子说，"可它倒使我觉得好饥饿。"说完她就叫着"嘎，嘎，嘎"朝下游泅水而去了。

"回来，快回来！"火箭尖声叫着，"我有好多话要对你说。"但是鸭子没理会他。"走了也好，"他对自己说，"她的思想的确只算得上一般。"他往稀泥中陷得更深了，这时才开始想起天才的寂寞来。忽然有两个小男孩身穿白色的粗布衫，手拿一只水壶，怀里抱着好些柴火，朝岸边跑了过来。

"这一定是代表团了。"火箭说着，又努力表现出非常庄重的样子。

"嘿！"其中的一个孩子叫道，"快看这根旧木棍！我不知道它怎么会在这儿。"他把火箭从阴沟里拾起。

"旧木棍！"火箭说，"不可能！金木棍，这才是他说的。金木棍才是很中听的话。实际上，他把我错当成宫中的某位显贵了。"

"我们把它放到火里去吧！"另一个孩子说，"多一把火烧水也好。"

于是他俩把柴火堆在一起，把火箭放在最上面，并点燃了火。

"这下可太棒了，"火箭大声叫道，"他们要在大白天里把我给燃放了，这样人人都会看见我了。"

"我们现在去睡觉吧，"他俩说，"睡醒时水壶的水就会烧开了。"说完他们便在草地上躺下身，闭上了眼睛。

火箭浑身都湿透了，所以花了好长时间才把他烤干。不过，到最后火苗还是把他点燃了。

"现在我就要升空了！"他大叫起来，同时把身体挺得笔直笔直的。"我知道我要飞得比星星更高，比月亮更高，比太阳更高。其实，我会飞得高到——"

嘶嘶！嘶嘶！嘶嘶！他垂直朝天空中飞去。

"太棒了！"他叫了起来，"我要这样一直飞下去，我是多么的成功啊！"

不过，没有人看见他。

这时他开始感到有一股奇怪的刺痛袭遍全身。

"现在我就要爆炸了，"他大声喊道，"我要点燃整个世界，我要声威大震，让所有的人在这一年里都不再谈论别的事情。"的确他真的爆炸了。呼！呼！呼！火药爆炸了。这是千真万确的。

可是没有人听见他，就连那两个小孩也没有听见，因为他俩睡得可熟了。

　　接着他所剩下的只有木棍了，木棍掉下去，正好落在一只在阴沟边散步的鹅的背上。

　　"天呀！"鹅叫了起来，"怎么下起棍子来了。"说完就跳进河里去了。

　　"我知道我会创造奇迹的。"火箭喘息着说，然后他就熄灭了。

The Remarkable Rocket

The King's son was going to be married, so there were general rejoicings. He had waited a whole year for his bride, and at last she had arrived. She was a Russian Princess, and had driven all the way from Finland in a sledge drawn by six reindeer. The sledge was shaped like a great golden swan, and between the swan's wings lay the little Princess herself. Her long ermine cloak reached right down to her feet, on her head was a tiny cap of silver tissue, and she was as pale as the Snow Palace in which she had always lived. So pale was she that as she drove through the streets all the people wondered. "She is like a white rose!" they cried, and they threw down flowers on her from the balconies.

At the gate of the Castle the Prince was waiting to receive her. He had dreamy violet eyes, and his hair was like fine gold. When he saw her he sank upon one knee, and kissed her hand.

"Your picture was beautiful," he murmured, "but you are more beautiful than your picture;" and the little Princess blushed.

"She was like a white rose before," said a young Page to his neighbour, "but she is like a red rose now;" and the whole Court was delighted.

For the next three days everybody went about saying, "White rose, Red rose, Red rose, White rose;" and the King gave orders that the Page's salary was to be doubled. As he received no salary at all this was not of much use to him, but it was considered a great honour, and was duly published in the Court Gazette.

When the three days were over the marriage was celebrated. It was a magnificent ceremony, and the bride and bridegroom walked hand in hand under a canopy of purple velvet embroidered with little pearls. Then there was a State Banquet, which lasted for five hours. The Prince and Princess sat at the top of the Great Hall and drank out of a cup of clear crystal. Only

夜
莺
与
玫
瑰

true lovers could drink out of this cup, for if false lips touched it, it grew grey and dull and cloudy.

"It's quite clear that they love each other," said the little Page, "as clear as crystal!" and the King doubled his salary a second time. "What an honour!" cried all the courtiers.

After the banquet there was to be a Ball. The bride and bridegroom were to dance the Rose-dance together, and the King had promised to play the flute. He played very badly, but no one had ever dared to tell him so, because he was the King. Indeed, he knew only two airs, and was never quite certain which one he was playing; but it made no matter, for, whatever he did, everybody cried out, "Charming! Charming!"

The last item on the programme was a grand display of fireworks, to be let off exactly at midnight. The little Princess had never seen a firework in her life, so the King had given orders that the Royal Pyrotechnist should be in attendance on the day of her marriage.

"What are fireworks like?" she had asked the Prince,

了不起的火箭

one morning, as she was walking on the terrace.

"They are like the Aurora Borealis," said the King, who always answered questions that were addressed to other people, "only much more natural. I prefer them to stars myself, as you always know when they are going to appear, and they are as delightful as my own flute-playing. You must certainly see them."

So at the end of the King's garden a great stand had been set up, and as soon as the Royal Pyrotechnist had put everything in its proper place, the fireworks began to talk to each other.

"The world is certainly very beautiful," cried a little Squib. "Just look at those yellow tulips. Why! If they were real crackers they could not be lovelier. I am very glad I have travelled. Travel improves the mind wonderfully, and does away with all one's prejudices."

"The King's garden is not the world, you foolish squib," said a big Roman Candle; "the world is an enormous place, and it would take you three days to see it thoroughly."

"Any place you love is the world to you," exclaimed a pensive Catherine Wheel, who had been attached to an old deal box in early life, and prided herself on her broken heart; "but love is not fashionable any more, the poets have killed it. They wrote so much about it that nobody believed them, and I am not surprised. True love suffers, and is silent. I remember myself once— But it is no matter now. Romance is a thing of the past."

"Nonsense!" said the Roman Candle, "Romance never dies. It is like the moon, and lives forever. The bride and bridegroom, for instance, love each other very dearly. I heard all about them this morning from a brown-paper cartridge, who happened to be staying in the same drawer as myself, and knew the latest Court news."

But the Catherine Wheel shook her head. "Romance is dead, Romance is dead, Romance is dead," she murmured. She was one of those people who think that, if you say the same thing over and over a great many times, it becomes true in the end.

了不起的火箭

141

Suddenly, a sharp, dry cough was heard, and they all looked round.

It came from a tall, supercilious-looking Rocket, who was tied to the end of a long stick. He always coughed before he made any observation, so as to attract attention.

"Ahem! Ahem!" he said, and everybody listened except the poor Catherine Wheel, who was still shaking her head, and murmuring, "Romance is dead."

"Order! Order!" cried out a Cracker. He was something of a politician, and had always taken a prominent part in the local elections, so he knew the proper Parliamentary expressions to use.

"Quite dead," whispered the Catherine Wheel, and she went off to sleep.

As soon as there was perfect silence, the Rocket coughed a third time and began. He spoke with a very slow, distinct voice, as if he was dictating his memoirs, and always looked over the shoulder of the person to whom he was talking. In fact, he had a most distinguished manner.

"How fortunate it is for the King's son," he remarked, "that he is to be married on the very day on which I am to be let off. Really, if it had been arranged beforehand, it could not have turned out better for him; but, Princes are always lucky."

"Dear me!" said the little Squib, "I thought it was quite the other way, and that we were to be let off in the Prince's honour."

"It may be so with you," he answered; "indeed, I have no doubt that it is, but with me it is different. I am a very remarkable Rocket, and come of remarkable parents. My mother was the most celebrated Catherine Wheel of her day, and was renowned for her graceful dancing. When she made her great public appearance she spun round nineteen times before she went out, and each time that she did so she threw into the air seven pink stars. She was three feet and a half in diameter, and made of the very best gunpowder. My father was a Rocket like myself, and of French extraction. He flew so high that the people were afraid that he would never come down again. He did, though, for he was of a kindly disposition, and he made a most brilliant descent in a shower of golden rain. The newspapers wrote about his performance in very flattering terms. Indeed, the Court Gazette called him a triumph of Pylotechnic art."

"Pyrotechnic, Pyrotechnic, you mean," said a Bengal Light; "I know it is Pyrotechnic, for I saw it written on my own canister."

"Well, I said Pylotechnic," answered the Rocket, in a severe tone of voice, and the Bengal Light felt so crushed that he began at once to bully the little squibs, in order to show that he was still a person of some importance.

"I was saying," continued the Rocket, "I was saying— What was I saying?"

"You were talking about yourself," replied the Roman Candle.

"Of course; I knew I was discussing some

interesting subject when I was so rudely interrupted. I hate rudeness and bad manners of every kind, for I am extremely sensitive. No-one in the whole world is so sensitive as I am, I am quite sure of that."

"What is a sensitive person?" said the Cracker to the Roman Candle.

"A person who, because he has corns himself, always treads on other people's toes," answered the Roman Candle in a low whisper; and the Cracker nearly exploded with laughter.

"Pray, what are you laughing at?" inquired the Rocket; "I am not laughing."

"I am laughing because I am happy," replied the Cracker.

"That is a very selfish reason," said the Rocket angrily. "What right have you to be happy? You should be thinking about others. In fact, you should be thinking about me. I am always thinking about myself, and I expect everybody else to do the same. That is what is called sympathy. It is a beautiful virtue, and I possess

了不起的火箭

145

it in a high degree. Suppose, for instance, anything happened to me tonight, what a misfortune that would be for every one! The Prince and Princess would never be happy again, their whole married life would be spoiled; and as for the King, I know he would not get over it. Really, when I begin to reflect on the importance of my position, I am almost moved to tears."

"If you want to give pleasure to others," cried the Roman Candle, "you had better keep yourself dry."

"Certainly," exclaimed the Bengal Light, who was now in better spirits; "that is only common sense."

"Common sense, indeed!" said the Rocket indignantly; "you forget that I am very uncommon, and very remarkable. Why, anybody can have common sense, provided that they have no imagination. But I have imagination, for I never think of things as they really are; I always think of them as being quite different. As for keeping myself dry, there is evidently no one here who can at all appreciate an emotional nature. Fortunately for myself, I don't care. The only thing that sustains one through life is the consciousness of the immense inferiority of everybody else, and this is a feeling that I have always cultivated. But none of you have any hearts. Here you are laughing and making merry just as if the Prince and Princess had not just been married."

"Well, really," exclaimed a small Fire-balloon, "why not? It is a most joyful occasion, and when I soar up into the air I intend to tell the stars all about it. You will see them twinkle when I talk to them about the pretty bride."

"Ah! what a trivial view of life!" said the Rocket; "But it is only what I expected. There is nothing in you; you are hollow and empty. Why, perhaps the Prince and Princess may go to live in a country where there is a deep river, and perhaps they may have one only son, a little fair-haired boy with violet eyes like the Prince himself; and perhaps some day he may go out to walk with his nurse; and perhaps the nurse may go to sleep under a great elder-tree; and

了
不
起
的
火
箭

perhaps the little boy may fall into the deep river and be drowned. What a terrible misfortune! Poor people, to lose their only son! It is really too dreadful! I shall never get over it."

"But they have not lost their only son," said the Roman Candle; "no misfortune has happened to them at all."

"I never said that they had," replied the Rocket; "I said that they might. If they had lost their only son there would be no use in saying anything more about the matter. I hate people who cry over spilt milk. But when I think that they might lose their only son, I certainly am very much affected."

"You certainly are!" cried the Bengal Light. "In fact, you are the most affected person I ever met."

"You are the rudest person I ever met," said the Rocket, "and you cannot understand my friendship for the Prince."

"Why, you don't even know him," growled the Roman Candle.

"I never said I knew him," answered the Rocket.

"I dare say that if I knew him I should not be his friend at all. It is a very dangerous thing to know one's friends."

"You had really better keep yourself dry," said the Fire-balloon. "That is the important thing."

"Very important for you, I have no doubt," answered the Rocket, "but I shall weep if I choose"; and he actually burst into real tears, which flowed down his stick like rain-drops, and nearly drowned two little beetles, who were just thinking of setting up house together, and were looking for a nice dry spot to live in.

"He must have a truly romantic nature," said the Catherine Wheel, "for he weeps when there is nothing at all to weep about;" and she heaved a deep sigh, and thought about the deal box.

But the Roman Candle and the Bengal Light were quite indignant, and kept saying, "Humbug! Humbug!" at the top of their voices. They were extremely practical, and whenever they objected to anything they called it humbug.

Then the moon rose like a wonderful silver shield; and the stars began to shine, and a sound of music came from the palace.

The Prince and Princess were leading the dance. They danced so beautifully that the tall white lilies peeped in at the window and watched them, and the great red poppies nodded their heads and beat time.

Then ten o'clock struck, and then eleven, and then twelve, and at the last stroke of midnight every one came out on the terrace, and the King sent for the Royal Pyrotechnist.

"Let the fireworks begin," said the King; and the Royal Pyrotechnist made a low bow, and marched down to the end of the garden. He had six attendants with him, each of whom carried a lighted torch at the end of a long pole.

It was certainly a magnificent display.

Whizz! Whizz! went the Catherine Wheel, as she spun round and round. Boom! Boom! went the Roman

Candle. Then the Squibs danced all over the place, and the Bengal Lights made everything look scarlet. "Good-bye," cried the Fire-balloon, as he soared away, dropping tiny blue sparks. Bang! Bang! answered the Crackers, who were enjoying themselves immensely. Every one was a great success except the Remarkable Rocket. He was so damp with crying that he could not go off at all. The best thing in him was the gunpowder, and that was so wet with tears that it was of no use. All his poor relations, to whom he would never speak, except with a sneer, shot up into the sky like wonderful golden flowers with blossoms of fire. Huzza! Huzza! cried the Court; and the little Princess laughed with pleasure.

"I suppose they are reserving me for some grand occasion," said the Rocket; "no doubt that is what it means," and he looked more supercilious than ever.

The next day the workmen came to put everything tidy. "This is evidently a deputation," said the Rocket; "I will receive them with becoming dignity," so he put

了
不
起
的
火
箭

151

his nose in the air, and began to frown severely as if he were thinking about some very important subject. But they took no notice of him at all till they were just going away. Then one of them caught sight of him. "Hallo!" he cried, "what a bad rocket!" and he threw him over the wall into the ditch.

"Bad Rocket? Bad Rocket?" he said, as he whirled through the air; "Impossible! Grand Rocket, that is what the man said. Bad and Grand sound very much the same, indeed they often are the same;" and he fell into the mud.

"It is not comfortable here," he remarked, "but no doubt it is some fashionable watering-place, and they have sent me away to recruit my health. My nerves are certainly very much shattered, and I require rest."

Then a little Frog, with bright jewelled eyes, and a green mottled coat, swam up to him.

"A new arrival, I see!" said the Frog. "Well, after all there is nothing like mud. Give me rainy weather and a ditch, and I am quite happy. Do you think it will be a wet afternoon? I am sure I hope so, but the sky is quite blue and cloudless. What a pity!"

"Ahem! Ahem!" said the Rocket, and he began to cough.

"What a delightful voice you have!" cried the Frog. "Really it is quite like a croak, and croaking is of course the most musical sound in the world. You will hear our glee-club this evening. We sit in the old duck pond close by the farmer's house, and as soon as the moon rises we begin. It is so entrancing that everybody lies awake to listen to us. In fact, it was only yesterday that I heard the farmer's wife say to her mother that she could not get a wink of sleep at night on account of us. It is most gratifying to find oneself so popular."

"Ahem! Ahem!" said the Rocket angrily. He was very much annoyed that he could not get a word in.

"A delightful voice, certainly," continued the Frog; "I hope you will come over to the duck-pond. I am off to

了不起的火箭

look for my daughters. I have six beautiful daughters, and I am so afraid the Pike may meet them. He is a perfect monster, and would have no hesitation in breakfasting off them. Well, good-bye: I have enjoyed our conversation very much, I assure you."

"Conversation, indeed!" said the Rocket. "You have talked the whole time yourself. That is not conversation."

"Somebody must listen," answered the Frog, "and I like to do all the talking myself. It saves time, and prevents arguments."

"But I like arguments," said the Rocket.

"I hope not," said the Frog complacently.

"Arguments are extremely vulgar, for everybody in good society holds exactly the same opinions. Good-bye a second time; I see my daughters in the distance;" and the little Frog swam away.

"You are a very irritating person," said the Rocket, "and very ill-bred. I hate people who talk about themselves, as you do, when one wants to talk about oneself, as I do. It is what I call selfishness, and selfishness is a most detestable thing, especially to any one of my temperament, for I am well known for my sympathetic nature. In fact, you should take example by me; you could not possibly have a better model. Now that you have the chance you had better avail yourself of it, for I am going back to Court almost immediately. I am a great favourite at Court; in fact, the Prince and Princess were married yesterday in my honour. Of course you know nothing of these matters, for you are a provincial."

"There is no good talking to him," said a Dragon-fly, who was sitting on the top of a large brown bulrush; "no good at all, for he has gone away."

"Well, that is his loss, not mine," answered the Rocket. "I am not going to stop talking to him merely because he pays no attention. I like hearing myself talk. It is one of my greatest pleasures. I often have long conversations all by myself, and I am so clever that sometimes I don't understand a single word of what I

了不起的火箭

am saying."

"Then you should certainly lecture on Philosophy," said the Dragon-fly; and he spread a pair of lovely gauze wings and soared away into the sky.

"How very silly of him not to stay here!" said the Rocket. "I am sure that he has not often got such a chance of improving his mind. However, I don't care a bit. Genius like mine is sure to be appreciated some day;" and he sank down a little deeper into the mud.

After some time a large White Duck swam up to him. She had yellow legs, and webbed feet, and was considered a great beauty on account of her waddle.

"Quack, quack, quack," she said. "What a curious shape you are! May I ask were you born like that, or is it the result of an accident?"

"It is quite evident that you have always lived in the country," answered the Rocket, "otherwise you would know who I am. However, I excuse your ignorance. It would be unfair to expect other people to be as remarkable as oneself. You will no doubt be surprised to hear that I can fly up into the sky, and come down in a shower of golden rain."

"I don't think much of that," said the Duck, "as I cannot see what use it is to any one. Now, if you could plough the fields like the ox, or draw a cart like the horse, or look after the sheep like the collie-dog, that would be something."

"My good creature," cried the Rocket in a very haughty tone of voice, "I see that you belong to the lower orders. A person of my position is never useful. We have certain accomplishments, and that is more than sufficient. I have no sympathy myself with industry of any kind, least of all with such industries as you seem to recommend. Indeed, I have always been of opinion that hard work is simply the refuge of people who have nothing whatever to do."

"Well, well," said the Duck, who was of a very peaceable disposition, and never quarrelled with any one, "everybody has different tastes. I hope, at any rate, that you are going to take up your residence here."

"Oh! dear no," cried the Rocket. "I am merely a visitor, a distinguished visitor. The fact is that I find this place rather tedious. There is neither society here, nor solitude. In fact, it is essentially suburban. I shall probably go back to Court, for I know that I am destined to make a sensation in the world."

"I had thoughts of entering public life once myself," remarked the Duck; "there are so many things that need reforming. Indeed, I took the chair at a meeting some time ago, and we passed resolutions condemning everything that we did not like. However, they did not seem to have much effect. Now I go in for domesticity, and look after my family."

"I am made for public life," said the Rocket, "and so are all my relations, even the humblest of them. Whenever we appear we excite great attention. I have not actually appeared myself, but when I do so it will be a magnificent sight. As for domesticity, it ages one rapidly, and distracts one's mind from higher things."

"Ah! the higher things of life, how fine they are!"
said the Duck; "and that reminds me how hungry I feel:"
and she swam away down the stream, saying, "Quack,
quack, quack."

"Come back! come back!" screamed the Rocket, "I
have a great deal to say to you;" but the Duck paid no
attention to him. "I am glad that she has gone," he said
to himself, "she has a decidedly middle-class mind;"
and he sank a little deeper still into the mud, and began
to think about the loneliness of genius, when suddenly
two little boys in white smocks came running down the
bank, with a kettle and some faggots.

"This must be the deputation," said the Rocket, and
he tried to look very dignified.

"Hallo!" cried one of the boys, "look at this old stick!
I wonder how it came here;" and he picked the rocket
out of the ditch.

"Old Stick!" said the Rocket, "Impossible! Gold
Stick, that is what he said. Gold Stick is very
complimentary. In fact, he mistakes me for one of

the Court dignitaries!"

"Let us put it into the fire!" said the other boy, "it will help to boil the kettle."

So they piled the faggots together, and put the Rocket on top, and lit the fire.

"This is magnificent," cried the Rocket, "they are going to let me off in broad day-light, so that every one can see me."

"We will go to sleep now," they said, "and when we wake up the kettle will be boiled;" and they lay down on the grass, and shut their eyes.

The Rocket was very damp, so he took a long time to burn. At last, however, the fire caught him.

"Now I am going off!" he cried, and he made himself very stiff and straight. "I know I shall go much higher than the stars, much higher than the moon, much higher than the sun. In fact, I shall go so high that—"

Fizz! Fizz! Fizz! and he went straight up into the air.

"Delightful!" he cried, "I shall go on like this for ever.

What a success I am!"

But nobody saw him.

Then he began to feel a curious tingling sensation all over him.

"Now I am going to explode," he cried. "I shall set the whole world on fire, and make such a noise that nobody will talk about anything else for a whole year." And he certainly did explode. Bang! Bang! Bang! went the gunpowder. There was no doubt about it.

But nobody heard him, not even the two little boys, for they were sound asleep.

Then all that was left of him was the stick, and this fell down on the back of a Goose who was taking a walk by the side of the ditch.

"Good heavens!" cried the Goose. "It is going to rain sticks;" and she rushed into the water.

"I knew I should create a great sensation," gasped the Rocket, and he went out.

了不起的火箭

161

少年国王

在加冕典礼的前一天晚上，少年国王独自一人坐在他那间漂亮的房子里。他的大臣们按照当时的礼节，头朝地向他鞠了躬，便告辞而去。他们来到皇宫的大厅中，向礼节教授学习最后的几堂课，因为他们当中有几个人的举止还没有经过教化，不用说，这是很不礼貌的事情。

这位少年——他仅仅是个少年，不过才十六岁——对他们的离去一点也不觉得难过。他把身体向后靠去，倒在他那绣花沙发的软垫上，长长地舒了一口气，他躺在那儿，睁着两眼，张着嘴，真像一位棕树林的牧神，又像一只被猎人刚刚抓获的森林中的小动物。

说来也巧，他正是猎人们找到的，他们遇到他也差不多是凭运气。当时他光着脚，手里拿着笛子，正跟在把他养大的穷牧羊人的羊群后面，而且他一直把自己看作穷牧羊人的儿子。

他的母亲原来是老国王的独生女儿。她偷偷地恋上

了一个比她地位低得多的人——有人说，那人是外地来的，他用笛子吹出魔术般的美妙声音，使年轻的公主钟情于他；另外有人说他是来自意大利里米尼的艺术家，公主对他很器重，也许是太看重他了。他不知怎的突然间从城市里消失了，他那幅没有完成的作品还留在大教堂里——那时小孩才一个星期大，就在母亲睡着的时候被人偷偷抱走，交给一对普通的农家夫妇去照管。这对夫妇自己没有孩子，住在密林的深处，从城里骑马要一天才能到达。不知是像宫廷的御医所宣布的那样因为悲伤过度，或者是像一些人所谈论的那样喝了放在香料酒中的一种意大利急性毒药，反正那位给予这孩子生命的苍白的少女在醒来不到一小时的时间就死去了。一位忠诚的差人带着孩子跨上马鞍走了，当他从疲惫的马背上俯下身来敲响牧羊人小茅屋简陋的房门时，公主的尸体正被下葬于一个打开的墓穴中，这个墓穴就挖在一个荒凉的教堂墓地里，那里靠近城门。据说在那个墓穴里还躺着另一具尸体，他是一位非常英俊的外地男人，他的双手被反绑着，打了个绳结，胸膛上有好多血淋淋的伤口。

至少，这正是人们私下悄悄相互传递的说法。然而令人确信的是老国王在临终时，不知是由于对自己犯下的大罪而悔恨，或是仅仅因为希望自己的王国不至于落入外人之手，就派人去找回那个孩子，并当着宫中大臣的面，承认孩子为自己的继位人。

似乎就从孩子被承认的那一刻起，他就表现出了对美丽事物的极大热情，这便注定了将对他的一生起到巨大的影响。伴随在他身侧的侍从们常常讲起，当他看见那些华丽的服装和贵重的宝石时会兴奋地大叫，并且在脱去身上的粗皮衣和粗羊皮外套时简直是欣喜若狂。有时候他确也很怀念他那段自由自在的森林生活，且始终都对占去一天大部分时间的繁杂的宫廷礼节感到愤懑，但这却是座富丽的宫殿——人们把它叫"逍遥宫"——此刻他一下子成了它的主人，对他来说，这就像是一个

专为取悦他而新建成的时髦的新世界；只要他能够从议会厅或会见室里逃出来，他便会跑下那立着镀金铜狮的亮闪闪的斑岩石大台阶，从一个屋子转到另一个屋子，又从一条走廊来到另一条走廊，好像要一个人在美中间找到一副止痛药，或一种治病的良方似的。

他把这称之为一种探险——说真的，对他来说这可是真正地在神境中漫游了。有时候会有几位身材苗条、身穿披风、飘着艳丽丝带的金发宫廷听差侍卫陪伴着；但更多的时候，他常常是一个人，凭着感觉上的某种敏捷的本能，这差不多是一种先见之明吧，把握到艺术的秘密最好是在秘密中求得，况且美也同智慧一样，钟爱的是孤独的崇拜者。

这段时期流传着很多有关他的奇闻怪事。据说有一位胖乎乎的市政长官，曾代表全城市民出来发表了一大通歌功颂德的话，他曾看见少年国王十分崇敬地跪在一幅刚从威尼斯带来的巨画面前，神情犹如朝拜天神。还有那么一次少年国王失踪了好几个小时，人们费了好大劲才在宫殿内北边小塔的一间小屋里找到了他，他正痴呆呆地凝视着一块刻有美少年阿多尼斯像的希腊宝石。还有人传说亲眼见他用自己的热唇去吻一座大理石古雕

像的前额，那座古雕像是人们在修建石桥时在河床中发现的，石像上还刻着罗马皇帝哈德良所拥有的比提尼亚奴隶的名字。他还花了一整夜时间去观察月光照在恩底弥翁银像上的各种变化。

一切稀罕的和昂贵的东西对他都有极大的吸引力，使他急切地想得到。为此他派出了许多商人，有的被派往北海，向那里的穷渔夫购买琥珀，有的到埃及去找寻那些只有在法老的墓穴中才能找到的绿宝石，据说这种宝石具有非同一般的魔力，还有的去波斯收购丝绒编织的地毯和彩陶，另外很多人去印度采购薄纱和着色的象牙，月亮宝石和翡翠手镯，檀香和蓝色珐琅以及细毛织披巾。

然而，最让他费心的还是在他登位加冕时穿的长袍。长袍是金线织的，另外还有嵌满了红宝石的王冠以及那根挂着一串串珍珠的权杖。的确，他今晚所想的就是这个，他躺在奢华的沙发上，望着大块的松木在壁炉中慢慢地燃尽。衣服的图样都是由那个时代最著名的艺术家亲手设计的，早在几个月前就呈交给他过目了，他也下了命令要求工匠们不分昼夜地把它们赶制出来，还让人去满世界找寻那些能够配得上他们手艺的珠宝。他在想象中看见自己穿着华贵的皇袍站在大教堂高高的祭坛上，他那孩子气的嘴唇上露出了笑容，那双森林人特有的黑眼睛也放射出明亮的光芒。

　　过了一会儿他站起身来，靠在壁炉顶部雕花的庇檐上，目光环视着灯光昏暗的屋子。四周的墙上挂着代表"美的胜利"的华丽挂毯。一个角落里，放着一架镶着玛瑙和蓝宝石的打字机。面对窗户立着一个异常别致的柜子，上面的漆格层不是镀了金粉就是镶着金片，格层上摆放着一些精美的威尼斯玻璃高脚酒杯，还有一个黑纹玛瑙大杯子。绸子的床单上绣着一些浅白的罂粟花，它们好像是从睡眠的倦手中撒落下来的。刻有条形凹槽的高大的象牙柱撑起天鹅绒的华盖，华盖上面大簇的鸵鸟毛像白色泡沫一般向上伸展，一直达到银白色的回纹装饰屋顶上。用青铜做的美少年纳西索斯像满脸笑容地用双手举起一面亮光光的镜子。桌上放着一个紫水晶做的碗。

窗外，他可以看见教堂的大圆顶，隐隐约约像个气泡浮动在阴暗的房屋上面。无精打采的哨兵们在靠近河边的雾蒙蒙的阳台上来回地走着。在远处的一座果园里，一只夜莺在唱歌。一阵淡淡的茉莉花香从开着的窗户飘了进来。他把自己的棕色卷发从前额朝后掠去，随后拿起一只鲁特琴，手指随便地在弦上拨弄着。他的眼皮沉重地往下垂去，一股莫名的倦意袭上身来。在这以前他从来没有这么强烈地并且是如此兴奋地感受到美的东西的魔力和神秘。

钟楼传来午夜钟声的时候，他按了一下铃，听差们进来了，按繁杂的礼节为他脱去袍子，并往他手上洒上玫瑰香水，在他的枕头上撒上鲜花。待他们退出房间后没多久，他就入睡了。

他睡着后做了一个梦，梦是这样的。

他觉得自己正站在一间又长又矮的阁楼里，四周是一片织布机的转动声和敲击声。微弱的光线透过格栅窗射了进来，他看见了那些俯在织机台上工作的织工们憔悴的身影。一些面带病容脸色苍白的孩子们蹲在巨大的

夜莺与玫瑰

横梁前面。每当梭子飞快地穿过丝线的时候，他们便把沉重压板拉起来，梭子一停下来，又立即把压板放下去，把线压在一起。他们的脸上露出饥饿难忍的表情，一双双干枯的手不停地颤抖着。一些憔悴的妇人坐在一张桌边缝着衣服。房间里充满了刺鼻的臭气，空气既污浊又沉闷，四壁因潮湿而滴水不止。

少年国王来到一位织工跟前，看着他工作。

织工却怒冲冲地望着他说："你为什么老看着我？你是不是主人派来监视我们干活的探子？"

"谁是你们的主人？"少年国王问道。

"我们的主人！"织工痛苦地大声说，"他是跟我一样的人。其实，我和他之间就这么点区别——他穿漂亮的衣服而我总是破衣烂衫，我饿得骨瘦如柴，他却饱得难受。"

"这是个自由的国家，"少年国王说，"你不是任何人的奴隶。"

"战争年代，"织工回答说，"强者把弱者变为奴隶，而在和平年代，富人把穷人变成奴隶。我们必须靠干活来糊口，可是他们给的工资少得可怜，我们会被饿死的。我们整天为他们做苦役，他们的箱子里堆满了黄金，我们的子女还未长大成人就夭折了，我们所爱的那些人的脸变得

少年国王

愁苦而凶恶。我们榨出的葡萄汁，却让别人去品尝。我们种出的谷物，却不能端上我们的饭桌。我们戴着枷锁，尽管它们是无形的；我们是奴隶，虽然人们说我们是自由人。"

"所有的人都是这样的吗？"少年国王问道。

"所有的人都这样，"织工答道，"不论是年轻的还是年老的，不管是男人还是女人，未成年的小孩子还是饱受生活打击的成人，都是这样。商人们压榨我们，我们还得照他们的话去做。牧师们骑马从我们身边走过，口中不停地数着念珠，没有一个人关心我们。'穷困'睁着饥饿的双眼爬过阴暗的小巷，'罪恶'面无表情地紧随其后。早晨唤醒我们的是'悲痛'，晚上伴我们入睡的是'耻辱'。但是这些与你有什么关系？你跟我们不是一个世界的人。你的神情是多么快乐啊！说完他满脸不高兴地转过头去，并把梭子穿过织机，少年国王看见梭子上面织出的是一根金线。"

他心中猛地一惊，赶紧问织工："你织的是什么袍子？"

"这是少年国王加冕时穿的袍子，"他回答说，"你问这干什么？"

这时，少年国王大叫一声便醒了，天啊！他原来是在自己的房间里，透过窗户他看见蜜色的大月亮正挂在迷雾般的夜空中。

他又一次睡着了，再次做起了梦，梦是这样的。

他觉得自己躺在一艘大帆船的甲板上面，一百个奴隶在为船划桨。船长就坐在他身边的地毯上。他黑得像一块乌木，头巾是深红色的丝绸做的。厚厚的耳垂上挂着一对硕大的银耳坠，手中拿着一杆象牙秤。

奴隶们除了腰间的一块破烂的遮羞布外，全身上下光溜溜的，全部一对一对地被锁链锁住。骄阳热辣辣地射在他们身上，黑人们在过道上跑来跑去的，皮鞭不停地抽打在他们身上。他们伸出干枯的双臂，在水中划动着沉重的桨。咸咸的海水从桨上飞溅起来。

最后他们来到一个小港湾，并开始测量水深。一阵微风从岸上吹来，给甲板和大三角帆蒙上了一层细细的红沙。三个阿拉伯人骑着野毛驴赶来，朝他们投来标枪。船长拿起一张弓，射中了他们其中一人的咽喉。那人重重地跌进了海浪之中，他的同伴仓皇逃走了。一位面蒙黄色纱巾的女子骑着骆驼慢慢地跟在后面，还不时地回头看看那具死尸。

黑人们抛了锚，降下了帆，纷纷来到舱底下，拿出一根长长的吊梯，梯下绑着铅锤。船长把绳梯从船侧扔下去，把梯的两端系在两根铁柱上面。这时，黑人们抓住一位最年轻的奴隶，打开了他的脚镣，并往他的鼻孔和耳朵里灌满蜡，还在他的腰间捆上了一块石头。他疲惫地爬下绳梯，便消失在海水中，入水的地方冒出了几个水泡。另外一些奴隶在一旁好奇地张望着。在船头上坐着一位驱赶鲨鱼的人，他在单调地击着鼓。

过了一会儿，下水的人从水中冒了上来，喘着粗气攀梯而上，右手拿着一颗珍珠。黑人们从他手中夺去珍珠，又把他推到海里。而其他奴隶们已靠在桨旁睡着了。

他上来了一次又一次，每次都带上一颗美丽的珍珠。船长把珍珠都过了秤，并把它们放进一只绿色皮革的小袋子中。

少年国王想说点什么，可是他的舌头好像被粘在了上腭，他的嘴唇也动弹不了。黑人们在彼此谈着话，并开始为一串明珠争吵起来。两只白鹤围绕着帆船飞个不停。

这时下水的人最后一次冒出水来，带上来的珍珠比霍尔木兹岛所有的珍珠都要美，因为它的形状如同一轮满月，比晨星还要亮。不过他的脸却苍白异常，他一头倒在甲板上，鲜血立即从他的耳朵和鼻孔中迸射而出。他只是颤抖了一下就再也动弹不了了。黑人们耸耸肩，把他的尸体抛向船舷外的海水中。

　　船长笑了，他伸出手去拿起那颗珍珠，他一边看着它，一边把它放在自己的前额上并鞠了一个躬。"它应该用来，"他说，"用来装饰少年国王的权杖。"说完他朝黑人们打了个手势示意起锚。

　　少年国王听到这里，突然大叫一声，便醒了过来，窗外已是晨光熹微，星光逐渐暗淡了。

　　他再一次入睡了，做了梦，梦是这样的。

　　他觉得自己正徘徊在一个阴森森的树林中，树上悬挂着奇怪的果子和美丽而有毒的鲜花。他经过的地方，毒蛇朝他嘶嘶地叫着，羽毛华丽的鹦鹉尖叫着从一根树枝飞到另一根树枝上。巨大的乌龟躺在热乎乎的泥潭中睡大觉。树上到处都是猴子和孔雀。

　　他走着走着，一直来到树林的边缘，在那儿他看见有好大一群人在一条干枯的河床上做苦役。他们像蚂蚁般地蜂拥至岩石上。他们在地上挖了好些深洞，并下到洞里去。他们中的一些人用大斧头开山劈石，另一些人在沙滩上摸索着。他们连根拔起仙人掌，踏过鲜红的花朵。他们忙来忙去，彼此叫喊着，没有一个人偷懒。

　　死亡和贪婪从洞穴的阴暗处注视着他们，死亡开口说：

少年国王

"我已经疲倦了，把他们中的三分之一给我，我要走了。"

不过贪婪却摇了摇头。"他们是我的仆人。"她回答说。

死亡对她说："你手中拿的是什么东西？"

"我有三粒谷子，"她回答说，"那跟你有什么关系？"

"给我一粒，"死亡大声说，"去种在我的花园中，只要一粒，我要走了。"

"我什么也不会给你的。"贪婪说，说着她把手藏在自己衣襟下面。

死亡笑了。他拿起一只杯子，把它浸在水池中，等杯子出来时里面已生出了疟疾。疟疾从人群中走过，三分之一的人便倒下死去了。疟疾的身后卷起一股寒气，身旁狂窜着无数条水蛇。

贪婪看见三分之一的人都死去了，便捶胸大哭起来。她捶打着自己干枯的胸膛，哭叫着说："你杀死了我三分之一的仆人，你快走吧。在鞑靼人的山里正有战事，双方的国王都在呼唤你去。阿富汗人杀掉了黑牛，正开往前线。他们用长矛刺盾牌，还戴上了铁盔。我的山谷对你有什么用，你没有必要待在这儿吧？你快走吧，不要再到这儿来了。"

"不，"死亡回答说，"除非你给我一粒谷子，否则我是不会走的。"

贪婪一下子捏紧自己的手,牙齿也咬得紧绷绷的。"我不会给你任何东西的。"她喃喃地说。

死亡笑了。他捡起一块黑色的石头,朝树林中扔去,从密林深处的野毒芹丛中走出了身穿火焰长袍的黑热病。黑热病从人群中走过,去触摸他们,凡是被她碰着的人都死去了。她脚下踏过的青草也跟着枯萎了。

贪婪颤抖起来,在额头上抹了些灰。"你太残忍了,"她叫着说,"你太残忍了。在印度的好多城市里正闹着饥荒,撒马尔罕的蓄水池也干枯了。埃及的好多城市里也在闹饥荒,蝗虫也从沙漠飞来了。尼罗河也快决堤了,牧师们正痛骂他们自己的神爱伊西斯和奥西里斯。到那些需要你的人那儿去吧,放过我的仆人吧。"

"不,"死亡回答说,"除非你给我一粒谷子,否则我是不会离开的。"

"我什么东西也不会给你。"贪婪说。

死亡再一次笑了,他将手放在嘴上在指缝中吹了一声口哨,只见一个女人从空中飞来。她的额头上印着"瘟疫"两个字,一群饥饿的老鹰在她身旁飞旋着。她用巨大的翅膀盖住了整个山谷,没有一个人能逃脱她的魔掌。

贪婪尖叫着穿过树林逃走了，死亡跨上他那匹红色的大马也飞驰而去，他的马跑得比风还快。

从山谷底部的稀泥中爬出无数条龙和有鳞甲的怪兽，一群胡狼也沿着沙滩跑来，并用鼻孔贪婪地吸着空气。

少年国王哭了，他说："这些人是谁？他们在寻找什么东西？"

"国王王冠上的红宝石。"站在他身后的一个人说。

少年国王吃了一惊，转过头去，看见一个朝圣者模样的人，那人手中拿着一面银镜。

他脸色变得苍白起来，并开口问道："哪一个国王？"

朝圣者回答说："看着这面镜子，你会看见他的。"

他朝镜子看去，见到的是他自己的面孔，他大叫了一声就惊醒了。灿烂的阳光洒满屋子，从外面花园和庭院的树上传来了鸟儿的歌唱。

御前侍臣和文武百官走进房来向他行礼，侍者给他拿来用金线编织的长袍，还把王冠和权杖放在他面前。

少年国王看着它们，它们美极了，比他以前见过的任何东西都要美。然而他还记得自己做的梦，于是便对大臣们说："把这些东西都拿走，我不会穿戴它们的。"

群臣感到很惊讶，有些人甚至笑了，因为他们认为

夜莺与玫瑰

国王是在开玩笑。

可是他再次严肃地对他们说:"把这些东西都拿开,不要让我见到它们。虽然今天是我加冕的日子,但是我不会穿戴它们的。因为我的这件长袍是在忧伤的织机上用痛苦的苍白的双手织出来的。红宝石的心是用鲜血染红的。珍珠里则隐匿着死亡的阴影。"接着他对他们讲述了自己的三个梦。

大臣们听完故事后,互相对视着,低声交谈说:"他一定是疯了,梦终究是梦,幻觉也终究是幻觉,它们不是真的,用不着在意。再说,那些为我们做工的人的生命又与我们有什么相干呢?难道一个人没有看见播种就不能吃面包,没有与种葡萄的人交谈过就不能喝葡萄酒了吗?"

御前侍臣对少年国王说道:"陛下,我恳求您把这些忧伤的念头抛开,穿上这件美丽的王袍,戴上这顶王冠吧。如果您不穿上王袍,人民怎么会知道您就是国王呢?"

少年国王望着他。"真是这样吗?"他问道,"如果我不穿王袍,他们就不会知道我是国王了吗?"

"他们不会认识您的,陛下。"御前侍臣大声说。

"我从前还以为真有那么一些带帝王之相的人,"少年国王回答说,"不过也许正如你所说的,然而我还是不穿这身王袍，而且也不戴这顶王冠，我要像进宫时那样走出宫去。"

然后他吩咐他们都离去，只留一个比他小一岁的侍者来陪他。在清水中沐浴后，他打开一个漆彩艳丽的木箱，从箱中他拿出皮衣和粗羊皮外套，这些都是当年他在山上放羊时穿过的。他穿上它们，手里又拿起那根粗大的牧羊杖。

这位小侍者吃惊地睁大一双蓝色的眼睛，笑着对他说："陛下，我看见你的长袍和权杖，可你的王冠在哪儿？"

少年国王从攀附在阳台上的野荆棘上折下一枝，把它弯曲成一个圆圈，放在了自己的头上。

"这就是我的王冠。"他回答说。

这样穿戴好后，他走出房间来到大殿中，许多贵族早已等候在此。

贵族们觉得很可笑，他们中有的人还对他叫道："陛下，臣民们等着见他们的国王，而您却让他们看到了一位乞丐。"另有一些人怒气冲冲地说："他使我们的国家蒙羞，不配做我们的国王。"然而，他一言不发，只是朝前走去，走下明亮的斑岩石阶，出了青铜大门，骑上自己的坐骑，朝教堂奔去，小侍者跟在他身旁跑着。

百姓们笑了，他们说："骑马走过的是国王的小丑。"

少
年
国
王

他们嘲笑着他。

　　而他却勒住马，开口说道："不，我就是国王。"于是他把自己的三个梦讲给了他们听。

　　一个人从人群中走出，他痛苦地对他说道："陛下，你不知道穷人的生活是从富人的奢侈中得来的吗？就是靠你们的富有我们才得以生存，是你们的恶习给我们带来了面包。给一个严厉的主子干活是很艰苦的，但若没有主子要我们干活，那会更艰苦。你以为乌鸦会养活我们吗？对这些事你会有什么良方吗？你会对买主说'你要用这么多钱来买'，而同时对卖主说'你要以这个价格卖'吗？我敢说你不会。所以回到你自己的宫中去，穿上你的高贵紫袍吧。你和我们以及我们遭受的痛苦有什么相干呢？"

　　"难道富人和穷人不是兄弟吗？"少年国王问道。

　　"是啊，"那人回答说，"那个有钱兄长的名字叫该隐。"

　　少年国王的眼里充满了泪水，他骑着马在百姓们的喃喃低语中走过，小侍者感到好害怕，就走开了。

　　他来到教堂的大门口时，卫兵们举起他们手中的戟对他说："你到这儿来干什么？除了国王，任何人不得入内。"

　　一听这话他气得满脸通红，便对他们说："我就是国王。"说完把他们的戟推开，就走进去了。

夜莺与玫瑰

老主教看见他穿一身牧羊人的衣服走了进来，吃惊地从宝座上站起来，迎上前去，对他说："我的孩子，这是国王的衣服吗？我用什么王冠为你加冕？又拿什么样的权杖放在你的手中呢？今天应该是个快乐的日子，而不应是一个自取其辱的日子。"

"难道快乐应该穿上由愁苦织成的衣服吗？"少年国王说。然后他对老主教讲了自己的三个梦。

主教听完了三个梦后，眉头紧锁，他说："孩子，我是个老人，已进入垂暮之年，我知道在这个大千世界里还有很多邪恶的东西。凶恶的土匪从山上下来，掳去无数小孩，把他们卖给摩尔人。狮子躺在草丛中等着过往的商队，准备扑咬骆驼。野猪将山谷中的庄稼连根拔起。狐狸咬着山上的葡萄藤。海盗们在海岸一带兴风作浪，焚烧渔船，掠夺渔网。盐沼地里的麻风病人，住在破茅草屋里，没有人愿意接近他们。乞丐们在大街上流浪，同狗一起争食吃。你能够让这些事情不出现吗？你愿意让麻风病人同你一起睡觉，让乞丐同你一起进餐吗？你会叫狮子听你的话，野猪服从你的命令吗？难道制造出这些苦难的上帝还不如你聪明吗？因此，我不会为你所做的事而赞扬你，我要求你骑马回你自己的王宫中，脸上要露出笑容，并穿上符合国王身份的衣服，我要用金王冠来为你加冕，我要把嵌满珍珠的权杖放在你的手中。至于你的那些梦，就不要再想它们了。这世上的负担已经太重了，是一个人难以承受的；人间的愁苦也太大了，不是一颗心所能负担的。"

"你居然在教堂里说这样的话！"少年国王说。他大步从主教身旁走过，登上祭坛的台梯，站到了基督像前。

他站在基督像前，在他的左手边和右手边分别放着华丽的金盆，装黄酒的圣杯和装圣油的瓶子。他跪在基督像下，巨大的蜡烛在珠光宝气的神座旁明亮地燃烧着，燃香的烟雾绕成一圈圈蓝色的轻烟飘向屋梁。他低下头去进行祈祷，那些身穿硬挺法衣的牧师们纷纷走下了祭坛。

突然，从外面的大街上传来了喧哗声，一群头戴羽缨的贵族们走了进来，他们手中握着出鞘的宝剑和闪光的钢制盾牌。"做梦的那个人在什么地方？"他们大声嚷道，"那位国王，就是那位打扮得像个乞丐，给我们的国家带来耻辱的男孩在什么地方？我们一定要杀了他，因为他不配统治我们。"

少年国王再一次低下头去祈祷，祷告完毕他便站起身来，转过头去悲伤地望着他们。

啊！看啊，阳光透过彩色的玻璃窗照在他的身上，光线在他的四周织出一件金袍，比那件为取悦于他而编织的王袍更加美丽。干枯的枝条怒放出鲜花，那是比珍珠还要洁白的百合花。干枯的荆棘也开花了，开放出比红宝石还要红的红玫瑰。比上等珍珠还洁白的百合花，花梗犹如光亮的银子。比红宝石更红的玫瑰，叶片犹如闪亮的黄金。

他身穿国王的衣服站在那里，珠宝镶嵌的神龛打开了，光芒四射的圣体匣里，水晶放出异常神奇的光。他身穿国王的衣服站在那里，那里就充满了上帝的荣光，连壁龛中的圣徒们也好像在动。身穿国王的华贵衣服，他站在了他们的面前，风琴奏出了乐曲，号手吹响了号，唱诗班的孩子们在放声歌唱。

百姓们敬畏地跪下来，贵族们收回宝剑并向少年国王行礼，主教大人的脸色变得苍白，双手颤抖不已。"给你加冕的人比我更伟大。"他大声说道，并跪倒在国王面前。

少年国王从高高的祭坛上走下来，穿过人群朝自己的皇宫走去。此时没有一个人敢看他的脸，因为那容貌就跟天使一样。

The Young King

It was the night before the day fixed for his coronation, and the young King was sitting alone in his beautiful chamber. His courtiers had all taken their leave of him, bowing their heads to the ground, according to the ceremonious usage of the day, and had retired to the Great Hall of the Palace, to receive a few last lessons from the Professor of Etiquette; there being some of them who had still quite natural manners, which in a courtier is, I need hardly say, a very grave offence.

The lad—for he was only a lad, being but sixteen years of age—was not sorry at their departure, and had flung himself back with a deep sigh of relief on the soft cushions of his embroidered couch, lying there, wild-eyed and open-mouthed, like a brown woodland Faun, or some young animal of the forest newly snared by the hunters.

少年国王

And, indeed, it was the hunters who had found him, coming upon him almost by chance as, bare-limbed and pipe in hand, he was following the flock of the poor goatherd who had brought him up, and whose son he had always fancied himself to be.

The child of the old King's only daughter by a secret marriage with one much beneath her in station—a stranger, some said, who, by the wonderful magic of his lute-playing, had made the young Princess love him; while others spoke of an artist from Rimini, to whom the Princess had shown much, perhaps too much honour, and who had suddenly disappeared from the city, leaving his work in the Cathedral unfinished— he had been, when but a week old, stolen away from his mother's side, as she slept, and given into the charge of a common peasant and his wife, who were without children of their own, and lived in a remote part of the forest, more than a day's ride from the town. Grief, or the plague, as the court physician stated, or, as some suggested, a swift Italian poison administered in a cup of spiced wine, slew, within an hour of her wakening, the white girl who had given him birth, and as the trusty messenger who bore the child across his saddle–bow, stooped from his weary horse and knocked at the rude door of the goatherd's hut, the body of the Princess was being lowered into an open grave that had been dug in a deserted churchyard, beyond the city gates, a grave where, it was said, that another body was also lying, that of a young man of marvellous and foreign beauty, whose hands were tied behind him with a knotted cord, and whose breast was stabbed with many red wounds.

Such, at least, was the story that men whispered to each other. Certain it was that the old King, when on his death–bed, whether moved by remorse for his great sin, or merely desiring that the kingdom should not pass away from his line, had had the lad sent for, and, in the presence of the Council, had acknowledged him as his heir.

And it seems that from the very first moment of his recognition he had shown signs of that strange passion for beauty that was destined to have so great

少年国王

an influence over his life. Those who accompanied him to the suite of rooms set apart for his service, often spoke of the cry of pleasure that broke from his lips when he saw the delicate raiment and rich jewels that had been prepared for him, and of the almost fierce joy with which he flung aside his rough leathern tunic and coarse sheepskin cloak. He missed, indeed, at times the fine freedom of his forest life, and was always apt to chafe at the tedious Court ceremonies that occupied so much of each day, but the wonderful palace—Joyeuse, as they called it—of which he now found himself lord, seemed to him to be a new world fresh-fashioned for his delight; and as soon as he could escape from the council-board or audience-chamber, he would run down the great staircase, with its lions of gilt bronze and its steps of bright porphyry, and wander from room to room, and from corridor to corridor, like one who was seeking to find in beauty an anodyne from pain, a sort of restoration from sickness.

Upon these journeys of discovery, as he would call

them—and, indeed, they were to him real voyages through a marvellous land, he would sometimes be accompanied by the slim, fair-haired Court pages, with their floating mantles, and gay fluttering ribands; but more often he would be alone, feeling through a certain quick instinct, which was almost a divination, that the secrets of art are best learned in secret, and that Beauty, like Wisdom, loves the lonely worshipper.

Many curious stories were related about him at this period. It was said that a stout Burgomaster, who had come to deliver a florid oratorical address on behalf of the citizens of the town, had caught sight of him kneeling in real adoration before a great picture that had just been brought from Venice, and that seemed to herald the worship of some new gods. On another occasion he had been missed for several hours, and after a lengthened search had been discovered in a little chamber in one of the northern turrets of the palace gazing, as one in a trance, at a Greek gem carved with the figure of Adonis[1]. He had been seen, so the tale ran, pressing his warm lips to the marble brow of an antique statue that had been discovered in the bed of the river on the occasion of the building of the stone bridge, and was inscribed with the name of the Bithynian[2] slave of Hadrian. He had passed a whole night in noting the effect of the moonlight on a silver image of Endymion[3].

All rare and costly materials had certainly a great fascination for him, and in his eagerness to procure them he had sent away many merchants, some to traffic for amber with the rough fisher-folk of the north seas, some to Egypt to look for that curious green turquoise which is found only in the tombs of kings, and is said to possess magical properties, some to Persia for silken carpets and painted pottery, and others to India to buy gauze and stained ivory, moonstones and bracelets of jade, sandal-

[1] Adonis 阿多尼斯，希腊神话中的植物神，身高九尺，拥有俊美精致的五官，每年死而复生，永远年轻、容颜不老。阿多尼斯是西方"美男子"的最早出处。
[2] Bithynian 比提尼亚，古国名，在小亚细亚北部。
[3] Endymion 恩底弥翁，希腊神话中的俊美少年，为月亮女神塞勒涅所钟爱。

wood and blue enamel and shawls of fine wool.

But what had occupied him most was the robe he was to wear at his coronation, the robe of tissued gold, and the ruby-studded crown, and the sceptre with its rows and rings of pearls. Indeed, it was of this that he was thinking tonight, as he lay back on his luxurious couch, watching the great pinewood log that was burning itself out on the open hearth. The designs, which were from the hands of the most famous artists of the time, had been submitted to him many months before, and he had given orders that the artificers were to toil night and day to carry them out, and that the whole world was to be searched for jewels that would be worthy of their work. He saw himself in fancy standing at the high altar of the cathedral in the fair raiment of a King, and a smile played and lingered about his boyish lips, and lit up with a bright lustre his dark woodland eyes.

After some time he rose from his seat, and leaning against the carved penthouse of the chimney, looked round at the dimly-lit room. The walls were hung with rich tapestries representing the Triumph of Beauty. A large

少年国王

press, inlaid with agate and lapis-lazuli, filled one corner, and facing the window stood a curiously wrought cabinet with lacquer panels of powdered and mosaiced gold, on which were placed some delicate goblets of Venetian glass, and a cup of dark-veined onyx. Pale poppies were embroidered on the silk coverlet of the bed, as though they had fallen from the tired hands of sleep, and tall reeds of fluted ivory bare up the velvet canopy, from which great tufts of ostrich plumes sprang, like white foam, to the pallid silver of the fretted ceiling. A laughing Narcissus[1] in green bronze held a polished mirror above its head. On the table stood a flat bowl of amethyst.

Outside he could see the huge dome of the cathedral, looming like a bubble over the shadowy houses, and the weary sentinels pacing up and down on the misty terrace by the river. Far away, in an orchard, a nightingale was singing. A faint perfume of jasmine came through the open window. He brushed his brown

---

❶ Narcissus　纳西索斯，希腊神话中河神刻斐与水泽女神利里俄珀之子。他是一位长相清秀的少年，只对自己水中的倒影爱慕不已，最终在顾影自怜中死去，该词比喻自恋的人。

curls back from his forehead, and taking up a lute❶, let his fingers stray across the cords. His heavy eyelids drooped, and a strange languor came over him. Never before had he felt so keenly, or with such exquisite joy, the magic and the mystery of beautiful things.

When midnight sounded from the clock-tower he touched a bell, and his pages entered and disrobed him with much ceremony, pouring rose-water over his hands, and strewing flowers on his pillow. A few moments after they had left the room, he fell asleep.

And as he slept he dreamed a dream, and this was his dream.

He thought that he was standing in a long, low attic, amidst the whir and clatter of many looms. The meagre daylight peered in through the grated windows, and showed him the gaunt figures of the weavers bending over their cases. Pale, sickly-looking children were crouched on the huge cross-beams. As the shuttles

---

❶ lute 诗琴，鲁特琴，14-17世纪使用较多的一种形似吉他的半梨形拨弦乐器。

dashed through the warp they lifted up the heavy battens, and when the shuttles stopped they let the battens fall and pressed the threads together. Their faces were pinched with famine, and their thin hands shook and trembled. Some haggard women were seated at a table sewing. A horrible odour filled the place. The air was foul and heavy, and the walls dripped and streamed with damp.

The young King went over to one of the weavers, and stood by him and watched him.

And the weaver looked at him angrily, and said, "Why art[1] thou[2] watching me? Art thou a spy set on us by our master?"

"Who is thy[3] master?" asked the young King.

"Our master!" cried the weaver, bitterly. "He is a man like myself. Indeed, there is but this difference between us—that he wears fine clothes while I go in rags, and that while I am weak from hunger he suffers not a little

---

❶ art   （古英语）同are。
❷ thou   （古英语）同you。
❸ thy   （古英语）同your。

from overfeeding."

"The land is free," said the young King, "and thou art no man's slave."

"In war," answered the weaver, "the strong make slaves of the weak, and in peace the rich make slaves of the poor. We must work to live, and they give us such mean wages that we die. We toil for them all day long, and they heap up gold in their coffers, and our children fade away before their time, and the faces of those we love become hard and evil. We tread out the grapes, and another drinks the wine. We sow the corn, and our own board is empty. We have chains, though no eye beholds them; and we are slaves, though men call us free."

"Is it so with all?" he asked.

"It is so with all," answered the weaver, "with the young as well as with the old, with the women as well as with the men, with the little children as well as with those who are stricken in years. The merchants grind us down, and we must do their bidding. The priest rides by and tells his beads, and no man has care of us. Through

少年国王

199

our sunless lanes creeps Poverty with her hungry eyes, and Sin with his sodden face follows close behind her. Misery wakes us in the morning, and Shame sits with us at night. But what are these things to thee? Thou art not one of us. Thy face is too happy."And he turned away scowling, and threw the shuttle across the loom, and the young King saw that it was threaded with a thread of gold.

And a great terror seized upon him, and he said to the weaver, "What robe is this that thou art weaving?"

"It is the robe for the coronation of the young King," he answered; "what is that to thee?"

And the young King gave a loud cry and woke, and lo[●]! he was in his own chamber, and through the window he saw the great honey-colored moon hanging in the dusky air.

And he fell asleep again and dreamed, and this was his dream.

He thought that he was lying on the deck of a

[●] lo （古英语）看啊，瞧。

huge galley that was being rowed by a hundred slaves. On a carpet by his side the master of the galley was seated. He was black as ebony, and his turban was of crimson silk. Great earrings of silver dragged down the thick lobes of his ears, and in his hands he had a pair of ivory scales.

The slaves were naked, but for a ragged loin-cloth, and each man was chained to his neighbor. The hot sun beat brightly upon them, and the negroes ran up and down the gangway and lashed them with whips of hide. They stretched out their lean arms and pulled the heavy oars through the water. The salt spray flew from the blades.

At last they reached a little bay, and began to take soundings. A light wind blew from the shore, and covered the deck and the great lateen sail with a fine red dust. Three Arabs mounted on wild asses rode out and threw spears at them. The master of the galley took a painted bow in his hand and shot one of them in the throat. He fell heavily into the surf, and his companions galloped away. A woman wrapped in a yellow veil followed slowly on a camel, looking back now and then at the dead body.

As soon as they had cast anchor and hauled down the sail, the negroes went into the hold and brought up a long rope–ladder, heavily weighted with lead. The master of the galley threw it over the side, making the ends fast to two iron stanchions. Then the negroes seized the youngest of the slaves, and knocked his gyves[1] oil, and filled his nostrils[2] and his ears with wax, and tied a big stone round his waist. He crept wearily down the ladder, and disappeared into the sea. A few bubbles rose where he sank. Some of the other slaves peered curiously over the side. At the prow of the galley sat a shark–charmer, beating monotonously upon a drum.

After some time the diver rose up out of the water, and clung panting to the ladder with a pearl in his right hand. The negroes seized it from him, and thrust him back. The slaves fell asleep over their oars.

Again and again he came up, and each time that he

夜莺与玫瑰

---

[1] gyve （古英语）脚铐，镣铐。
[2] nostril （拉丁文）鼻孔。

did so he brought with him a beautiful pearl. The master of the galley weighed them, and put them into a little bag of green leather.

The young King tried to speak, but his tongue seemed to cleave to the roof of his mouth, and his lips refused to move. The negroes chattered to each other, and began to quarrel over a string of bright beads. Two cranes flew round and round the vessel.

Then the diver came up for the last time, and the pearl that he brought with him was fairer than all the pearls of Ormuz, for it was shaped like the full moon, and whiter than the morning star. But his face was strangely pale, and as he fell upon the deck the blood gushed from his ears and nostrils. He quivered for a little, and then he was still. The negroes shrugged their shoulders, and threw the body overboard.

And the master of the galley laughed, and, reaching out, he took the pearl, and when he saw it he pressed it to his forehead and bowed. "It shall be," he said, "for the sceptre of the young King," and he made a sign to the

少年国王

203

negroes to draw up the anchor.

And when the young King heard this he gave a great cry, and woke, and through the window he saw the long grey fingers of the dawn clutching at the fading stars.

And he fell asleep again, and dreamed, and this was his dream.

He thought that he was wandering through a dim wood, hung with strange fruits and with beautiful poisonous flowers. The adders hissed at him as he went by, and the bright parrots flew screaming from branch to branch. Huge tortoises lay asleep upon the hot mud. The trees were full of apes and peacocks.

On and on he went, till he reached the outskirts of the wood, and there he saw an immense multitude of men toiling in the bed of a dried-up river. They swarmed up the crag like ants. They dug deep pits in the ground and went down into them. Some of them cleft the rocks with great axes; others grabbled in the sand. They tore up the cactus by its roots, and trampled on the scarlet blossoms. They hurried about, calling to each other, and no man was idle.

From the darkness of a cavern Death and Avarice watched them, and Death said, "I am weary; give me a third of them and let me go."

But Avarice shook her head. "They are my servants," she answered.

And Death said to her, "What hast thou in thy hand?"

"I have three grains of corn," she answered; "what is that to thee?"

"Give me one of them," cried Death, "to plant in my garden; only one of them, and I will go away."

"I will not give thee❶ anything," said Avarice, and she hid her hand in the fold of her raiment.

And Death laughed, and took a cup, and dipped it into a pool of water, and out of the cup rose Ague. She passed through the great multitude, and a third of them lay dead. A cold mist followed her, and the water-snakes ran by her side.

---

❶ thee （古英语）同 you（宾格）。

And when Avarice saw that a third of the multitude was dead she beat her breast and wept. She beat her barren bosom and cried aloud. "Thou hast slain a third of my servants," she cried, "get thee gone. There is war in the mountains of Tartary, and the kings of each side are calling to thee. The Afghans have slain the black ox, and are marching to battle. They have beaten upon their shields with their spears, and have put on their helmets of iron. What is my valley to thee, that thou shouldst[1] tarry in it? Get thee gone, and come here no more."

"Nay," answered Death, "but till thou hast given me a grain of corn I will not go."

But Avarice shut her hand, and clenched her teeth. "I will not give thee anything," she muttered.

And Death laughed, and took up a black stone, and threw it into the forest, and out of a thicket of wild hemlock came Fever in a robe of flame. She passed through the multitude, and touched them, and each man that she touched died. The grass withered beneath

---

❶ shouldst　（古英语）同should。

her feet as she walked.

And Avarice shuddered, and put ashes on her head. "Thou art cruel," she cried; "thou art cruel. There is famine in the walled cities of India, and the cisterns of Samarcand have run dry. There is famine in the walled cities of Egypt, and the locusts have come up from the desert. The Nile has not overflowed its banks, and the priests have cursed Isis[1] and Osiris[2]. Get thee gone to those who need thee, and leave me my servants."

"Nay," answered Death, "but till thou hast given me a grain of corn I will not go."

"I will not give thee anything," said Avarice.

And Death laughed again, and he whistled through his fingers, and a woman came flying through the air. Plague was written upon her forehead, and a crowd of lean vultures wheeled round her. She covered the valley with her wings, and no man was left alive.

And Avarice fled shrieking through the forest, and Death leaped upon his red horse and galloped away,

---

[1] Isis　伊西斯，埃及神话中古埃及掌管生育和繁殖的女神。
[2] Osiris　奥西里斯，埃及神话中伊希斯的丈夫，死后是地界主宰死亡的判官。

and his galloping was faster than the wind.

And out of the slime at the bottom of the valley crept dragons and horrible things with scales, and the jackals came trotting along the sand, sniffing up the air with their nostrils.

And the young King wept, and said: "Who were these men and for what were they seeking?"

"For rubies for a king's crown," answered one who stood behind him.

And the young King started, and, turning round, he saw a man habited as a pilgrim and holding in his hand a mirror of silver.

And he grew pale, and said: "For what king?"

And the pilgrim answered: "Look in this mirror, and thou shalt❶ see him."

And he looked in the mirror, and, seeing his own face, he gave a great cry and woke, and the bright sunlight was streaming into the room, and from the trees of the garden and pleasaunce the birds were singing.

❶ shalt （古英语）同shall。

And the Chamberlain and the high officers of State came in and made obeisance to him, and the pages brought him the robe of tissued gold, and set the crown and the sceptre before him.

And the young King looked at them, and they were beautiful. More beautiful were they than aught[1] that he had ever seen. But he remembered his dreams, and he said to his lords: "Take these things away, for I will not wear them."

And the courtiers were amazed, and some of them laughed, for they thought that he was jesting.

But he spake[2] sternly to them again, and said: "Take these things away, and hide them from me. Though it be the day of my coronation, I will not wear them. For on the loom of Sorrow, and by the white hands of Pain, has this my robe been woven. There is Blood in the heart of the ruby, and Death in the heart of the pearl." And he told them his three dreams.

And when the courtiers heard them they looked at each other and whispered, saying: "Surely he is mad; for

少年国王

---

[1] aught （古英语）任何事物。
[2] spake speak过去式，常用于诗歌，文学作品中。

what is a dream but a dream, and a vision but a vision? They are not real things that one should heed them. And what have we to do with the lives of those who toil for us? Shall a man not eat bread till he has seen the sower, nor drink wine till he has talked with the vinedresser?"

And the Chamberlain spake to the young King, and said, "My lord, I pray thee set aside these black thoughts of thine❶, and put on this fair robe, and set this crown upon thy head. For how shall the people know that thou art a king, if thou hast not a king's raiment?"

And the young King looked at him. "Is it so, indeed?" he questioned. "Will they not know me for a king if I have not a king's raiment?"

"They will not know thee, my lord," cried the Chamberlain.

"I had thought that there had been men who were kinglike," he answered, "but it may be as thou sayest❷. And yet I will not wear this robe, nor will I be crowned with this crown, but even as I came to the palace so

夜
莺
与
玫
瑰

❶ thine （古英语）同yours。
❷ sayest （古英语）say的第二人称单数。

will I go forth from it."

And he bade them all leave him, save one page whom he kept as his companion, a lad a year younger than himself. Him he kept for his service, and when he had bathed himself in clear water, he opened a great painted chest, and from it he took the leathern tunic and rough sheepskin cloak that he had worn when he had watched on the hillside the shaggy goats of the goatherd. These he put on, and in his hand he took his rude shepherd's staff.

And the little page opened his big blue eyes in wonder, and said smiling to him, "My lord, I see thy robe and thy sceptre, but where is thy crown?"

And the young King plucked a spray of wild briar that was climbing over the balcony, and bent it, and made a circlet of it, and set it on his own head.

"This shall be my crown," he answered.

And thus attired he passed out of his chamber into the Great Hall, where the nobles were waiting for him.

And the nobles made merry, and some of them

cried out to him, "My lord, the people wait for their king, and thou showest them a beggar," and others were wroth and said, "He brings shame upon our state, and is unworthy to be our master." But he answered them not a word, but passed on, and went down the bright porphyry staircase, and out through the gates of bronze, and mounted upon his horse, and rode towards the cathedral, the little page running beside him.

And the people laughed and said, "It is the King's fool who is riding by," and they mocked him.

And he drew rein and said, "Nay, but I am the King." And he told them his three dreams.

And a man came out of the crowd and spake bitterly to him, and said, "Sir, knowest thou not that out of the luxury of the rich cometh[1] the life of the poor? By your pomp we are nurtured, and your vices give us bread. To toil for a hard master is bitter, but to have no master to toil for is more bitter still. Thinkest[2] thou that the ravens will feed us? And what cure hast thou for these things?

[1] cometh （古英语）同come。
[2] thinkest （古英语）同think。

Wilt thou say to the buyer, 'Thou shalt buy for so much,' and to the seller, 'Thou shalt sell at this price?' I trow[1] not. Therefore go back to thy Palace and put on thy purple and fine linen. What hast thou to do with us, and what we suffer?"

"Are not the rich and the poor brothers?" asked the young King.

"Aye," answered the man, "and the name of the rich brother is Cain[2]."

And the young King's eyes filled with tears, and he rode on through the murmurs of the people, and the little page grew afraid and left him.

And when he reached the great portal of the cathedral, the soldiers thrust their halberts out and said, "What dost thou seek here? None enters by this door but the King."

And his face flushed with anger, and he said to them, "I am the King," and waved their halberts aside and passed in.

And when the old Bishop saw him coming in his goatherd's dress, he rose up in wonder from his throne, and

---

[1] trow 　（古英语）想，相信。
[2] Cain 　该隐，《圣经》中亚当与夏娃之长子，其弟亚伯的谋杀者。

went to meet him, and said to him, "My son, is this a king's apparel? And with what crown shall I crown thee, and what sceptre shall I place in thy hand? Surely this should be to thee a day of joy, and not a day of abasement."

"Shall Joy wear what Grief has fashioned?" said the young King. And he told him his three dreams.

And when the Bishop had heard them he knit his brows, and said, "My son, I am an old man, and in the winter of my days, and I know that many evil things are done in the wide world. The fierce robbers come down from the mountains, and carry off the little children, and sell them to the Moors. The lions lie in wait for the caravans, and leap upon the camels. The wild boar roots up the corn in the valley, and the foxes gnaw the vines upon the hill. The pirates lay waste the sea-coast and burn the ships of the fishermen, and take their nets from them. In the salt-marshes live the lepers; they have houses of wattled reeds, and none may come nigh them. The beggars wander through the cities, and eat their food with the dogs. Canst[1] thou make these things not to be? Wilt[2] thou take the leper for thy bedfellow, and set the beggar at thy board? Shall the lion do thy bidding, and the wild boar obey thee? Is not He who made misery wiser than thou art? Wherefore I praise thee not for this that thou hast done, but I bid thee ride back to the Palace and make thy face glad, and put on the raiment that beseemeth a king, and with the crown of gold I will crown thee, and the sceptre of pearl will I place in thy hand. And as for thy dreams, think no more of them. The burden of this world is too great for one man to bear, and the world's sorrow too heavy for one heart to suffer."

"Sayest thou that in this house?" said the young King, and he strode past the Bishop, and climbed up the steps of the altar, and stood before the image of Christ.

He stood before the image of Christ, and on his right hand and on his left were the marvellous vessels of gold, the chalice with the yellow wine, and the vial with the holy oil. He knelt before the image of Christ, and the great

---

① canst （古英语）同can。
② wilt （古英语）同will。

少年国王

candles burned brightly by the jewelled shrine, and the smoke of the incense curled in thin blue wreaths through the dome. He bowed his head in prayer, and the priests in their stiff copes crept away from the altar.

And suddenly a wild tumult came from the street outside, and in entered the nobles with drawn swords and nodding plumes, and shields of polished steel. "Where is this dreamer of dreams?" they cried. "Where is this King, who is apparelled like a beggar—this boy who brings shame upon our state? Surely we will slay him, for he is unworthy to rule over us."

And the young King bowed his head again, and prayed, and when he had finished his prayer he rose up, and turning round he looked at them sadly.

And lo! through the painted windows came the sunlight streaming upon him, and the sunbeams wove round him a tissued robe that was fairer than the robe that had been fashioned for his pleasure. The dead staff blossomed, and bare lilies that were whiter than pearls. The dry thorn blossomed, and bare roses that were redder than rubies. Whiter than fine pearls were the lilies, and their stems were of bright silver. Redder than male rubies were the roses, and their leaves were of beaten gold.

He stood there in the raiment of a king, and the gates of the jewelled shrine flew open, and from the crystal of the many-rayed monstrance shone a marvellous and mystical light. He stood there in a king's raiment, and the Glory of God filled the place, and the saints in their carven niches seemed to move. In the fair raiment of a king he stood before them, and the organ pealed out its music, and the trumpeters blew upon their trumpets, and the singing boys sang.

And the people fell upon their knees in awe, and the nobles sheathed their swords and did homage, and the Bishop's face grew pale, and his hands trembled. "A greater than I hath❶ crowned thee," he cried, and he knelt before him.

And the young King came down from the high altar, and passed home through the midst of the people. But no man dared look upon his face, for it was like the face of an angel.

---

❶ hath　（古英语）同have。

星星男孩

很久以前，有两个可怜的樵夫在松树林中寻找着回家的路。那是一个寒冷的冬夜，地上覆盖着厚厚的积雪，树枝也裹上了银装。在他们经过时，两旁被霜冻的小枝丫不断发出咔嚓断裂的声响。当他们来到山谷里，一股激流如同白练静静地悬挂在空中，因为冰之王亲吻了她，严寒把瀑布都冻结了！

这一夜实在是太冷了，就连鸟兽也不知道该怎么办才好。

"噢！"狼一边叫着，一边夹着尾巴从灌木丛一瘸一拐地走出来，"这真是倒霉的天气，政府为什么不想想办法呢？"

"啾！啾！啾！"绿色梅花雀喳喳地叫道，"年迈的地球已经死了，她被裹上白色的寿衣装殓了。"

"地球要出嫁了，这是她的婚纱。"斑鸠们在一起彼此悄悄地说。他们的小红脚都被冻坏了，不过他们觉得自己有责任用乐观浪漫的看法看待这一切。

"胡说！"狼咆哮着说，"我告诉你们这都是政府的过错，如果你们不相信我的话，我就吃掉你们。"狼十分注重实际，而且争论从未输过。

　　"嗯，就我个人而言，"啄木鸟说，他是一个天生的哲学家，"我不喜欢这种理论式的解释。如果一件事是什么样子，那么就本该如此，而眼下，这天气的确是太冷了。"

　　天气的确是冷透了。住在高高杉树上的小松鼠们互相摩擦着鼻子来取暖，野兔们在自己的洞中蜷缩着身子，甚至不敢朝外看上一眼。唯一好像欢喜这种天气的只有猫头鹰了。他们的羽毛让白霜冻得硬邦邦的，不过他们并不在意，他们不停地转动着他们那又大又黄的眼睛，隔着林子彼此呼唤着，"吐威特！吐伙！吐威特！吐伙！今天的天气多么好呀！"

两个樵夫继续不停地往前赶着路，并起劲地朝自己的手上吹热气，铁钉靴在雪地上留下一个个脚印。有一次他们陷进了一个深深的雪坑里，等他们出来的时候浑身上下白得就跟磨房的磨面师一样，这时石头也是很滑的；有一次他们在坚硬光滑的冰上跌倒了，这冰是沼泽地的水结成的，他们身上的柴捆跌落了，他们只好拾起来，重新捆绑好；还有一次他们以为自己迷了路，心中害怕得不得了，因为他们深知雪对那些睡在她怀中的人是很残酷的。不过他们信任那位好心的圣马丁（司旅行之神），他会照顾所有出门的人，于是他们又照来路退回，小心翼翼地迈着脚步，最后他们终于来到了森林的出口处，并看见下面山谷的远处，他们所在村庄亮着的灯光。

发现自己已脱离了险境，他俩真是欣喜若狂，高兴得大笑起来，大地在他们眼中就好像是一朵银色的花，月亮如同一朵金色的花。

然而笑过之后，他们又陷入了忧愁，因为他们想起了自己的穷困，一个樵夫对另一个说："我们为什么要高兴呢？要知道生活是为有钱人准备的，不是为我们这样的穷人准备的。我们还不如冻死在森林中呢，或者让野兽抓住把我们咬死。"

"真是如此，"他的伙伴回答说，"有些人享有的太多了，而另一些人却得到的太少了。不公平把世界分成两个样子了，可是除了忧愁之外，没有一件东西是可以公平分配的。"

可是，就在他们相互悲叹各自的不幸生活时，一件奇怪的事情发生了。从天上掉下来一颗非常明亮、非常美丽的星星。它经过其他星星的身旁，从天边滑落了下来，他们惊讶地望着它，在他们看来它似乎就落在小羊圈旁边不到一箭之遥的一丛柳树的后面。

"啊！找到的人说不定可以得到一坛子黄金！"他们惊叫着，跑了出去，他们太想得到黄金了。

其中一人跑得快一些，他超过了同伴，奋力穿过柳树，来到了树的另一边。呀！在雪地上的确有一个闪闪发光的东西。他急忙赶过去，弯下身用手去摸，那是一件用金线织的斗篷，上面精心地绣着好多星星，层层相叠，好像包裹了什么东西。他大声地对自己的同伴说他已经找到了从天上掉下来的财宝，等他的同伴走近时，他俩就在雪地上坐下来，打开斗篷，准备把金子拿出来平分。但是，啊呀！里面没有黄金，也没有白银，什么宝物都没有，只有一个熟睡的孩子。

其中一人对另外一人说："我们的希望竟是这样一个痛苦的结局，我们的运气不会好了，一个孩子对一个人会有什么好处呢？让我们离开这儿，走我们的路吧，要知道我们都是穷人，都有自己的孩子，我们不能把自己孩子的面包分给别人的孩子。"

不过他的同伴却回答他："不，把孩子丢在雪地里冻死，是不可饶恕的罪过，尽管我跟你一样的穷，还要养活好几口人，锅里又没有什么吃的东西，但是我还是要带他回家，我的妻子会照顾他的。"

他非常慈爱地抱起小孩，用斗篷包住孩子以抵御严寒，然后就下山回村子里去了，他的同伴对他的傻气和仁慈非常惊讶。

他们回到村里，他的同伴对他说："你有了这个孩子，那么把斗篷给我吧，因为我们都知道这应该平分的。"

然而他回答说："不，因为这个斗篷既不是你的，也不是我的，它是孩子的。"他与同伴道了别，来到自家的门前，敲起门来。

他的妻子打开门，看见自己的丈夫平安回来，就伸出双臂搂住他的脖子，吻着他，并从他背后取下柴捆，刷去他靴子上的雪，吩咐他快进屋去。

不过他对她说："我在森林中找到一样东西，我把他带回来好让你照顾他。"他站在门口并不进来。

"它是什么呀？"她大声问道，"快给我看看，家里是空荡荡的，我们正需要好多东西。"他把斗篷向后拉开，把熟睡的孩子抱给她看。

"唉哟，我的天！"她喃喃地说，"难道我们自己的孩子还不够多吗？干嘛非要再带一个回来凑热闹？谁知道他会不会给我们带来噩运？我们又拿什么来喂他呢？"她生气了。

"别生气，他可是一个星星男孩呀。"他回答说，他便把发现孩子的奇异经历讲给她听了。

不过她一点也没有消气，而是挖苦他，气愤地说道："我们孩子都没有面包吃，难道还要养别人的孩子吗？谁又来照顾我们呢？谁又给我们食物吃呢？"

"不要这样，上帝连麻雀都要照顾的，不会让它们饿死。"他回答说。

"麻雀在冬天不是常会饿死吗？"她问道，"现在不就是冬天吗？"她丈夫无言以对，只是站在门口不进屋来。

一阵寒风从树林刮来透过开着的大门，冷冷地灌进屋里。她打了一个寒战，哆嗦起来，并对他说："你不想把门关上吗？屋里吹进一股冷风了，我觉得好冷。"

"铁石心肠的人家，不是总有冷风吹进来吗？"他反问道。女人没有回答他，只是朝炉火靠得更近了。

过了一会儿她转过身来，望着他，她的眼里充满了泪水。他一下子冲了进来，把孩子放在她怀中，她吻了吻孩子，又把他放在一张小床上面，和他们最小的孩子睡在一起。

第二天，樵夫取下那件珍奇的金斗篷，把它放在一个大柜子中，他妻子也从孩子脖子上取下戴着的琥珀项链，一起收进柜中。

就这样，星星男孩跟樵夫的孩子一块儿长大了，他们坐在一起吃饭，又一起玩耍。他长得一年比一年英俊，住在村子里的人都为此而感到吃惊，因为大家又粗又黑，唯独他长得又白又娇嫩，就像精细的象牙一样，他的卷发如同水仙花环。他的嘴唇像红色的花瓣，他的双眼犹如清水河旁的紫罗兰，他的身体恰似田野中未经割除的百合一样圣洁。

不过他的美貌却给他带来了噩运。他因此变得骄傲、残酷和自私了。对于樵夫的儿女以及村子里的其他孩子们，他都一概瞧不起，并说他们出身低微，他认为自己是高贵的，是从星星里蹦出来的，他自认是他们的主人，叫人家做他的仆役。他一点也不怜悯穷人，也不怜悯那些残障人士以及任何有病苦的人，反而对他们扔石头，或赶他们到大路上去，命令他们到别处去乞讨，因此只有那些二流子才会第二次到那个村子去乞食。他也的确是迷恋自己的美，嘲弄那些孱弱和丑陋的人，不把他们当回事。对他自己却是爱得要命，在夏季无风的时候，他会躺在神父果园中的水井旁，朝井中望着自己俊俏的脸蛋，并为自己的美丽而高兴得笑起来。

樵夫和他的妻子常常责备他说："我们并未像你对待那些孤苦的人那样对待过你，你为什么会如此残酷地对待那些需要怜悯的可怜人呢？"

老神父也经常去找他，试图教他学会一些对事物的爱心，总对他说："苍蝇也是你的弟兄。不要去伤害它。那些在林中飞行的野鸟有它们的自由。不要抓它们来取乐。上帝创造了蜥蜴和鼹鼠，它们各自都有存在的价值。你是什么人，可以给上帝的世界带来痛苦？就连在农田中的牲畜都知道赞美上帝。"

可是星星男孩并不理睬他的话，他皱紧眉头，一副藐视的模样，又回去找他的伙伴，去领着他们玩了。他

的伙伴们也都跟随着他，因为他长得美，且脚步轻快，能够跳舞，还会吹笛子和弹奏音乐，不论星星男孩领他们去什么地方，他们都会去，不论星星男孩吩咐他们做什么，他们都会去做。他把一根尖芦苇刺进鼹鼠眼睛的时候，他们都开心地大笑；他用石头扔麻风病人时，他们也跟着大笑。无论他支配他们去干什么，他们都会变得跟他一样的铁石心肠。

有一天，一个可怜的要饭的女人走过村子。她的衣服破破烂烂的，一双脚因走了很多山路而鲜血淋淋，模样十分狼狈。因为太疲倦了，她就坐在栗子树下休息。

星星男孩看见她后，便对他的同伴们说："快看！这么一个肮脏的讨饭女人竟然坐在那棵美丽的绿叶树下面。来吧，我们把她赶走，她真是又丑又烦人。"

于是他走了过去朝她扔石头，嘲弄她，她用惊恐的眼光望着他，目不转睛地望着他。樵夫正在附近砍柴，看见了星星男孩的所作所为，他便跑上前来责备他："你的心真是太狠了，没有一点怜悯之心，这个可怜的女人对你做了什么坏事，你为什么要如此地对待她呢？"

星星男孩气得满脸通红，用脚猛跺着地面，并说道："你是什么人，敢来问我？我不是你的儿子，不会听你的话的。"

"你说的一点不假，"樵夫回答说，"但是当我在林中发现你时，我对你不也是动了怜悯之心吗？"

女人听到这些话后大叫了一声，昏倒在地上。樵夫把她扶进了自己的家中，他的妻子来照看她，等她从昏迷中醒过来之后，他们为她拿来了吃的和喝的，并吩咐她放宽心。

可是她既不肯吃，也不肯喝，只是对樵夫说："你不是说那个孩子是从林中捡来的吗？是不是十年前今天的事？"

樵夫回答说："是呀，我是在林中发现他的，就是十年前的今天。"

"发现他时有什么记号吗？"她大声问道，"他的脖子上是不是戴了一串琥珀项链？他的身上是不是包了一件绣着星星的金线斗篷？"

"就是这样，"樵夫回答说，"就跟你说的一模一样。"他从柜子中拿出放在那儿的斗篷和琥珀项链给她看。

她一看见这些东西，高兴得哭了起来，说道："他就是我丢失在林中的小儿子。我求你快叫他来，为了寻找他，我已经走遍了整个世界。"

樵夫和他的妻子赶紧走出去，叫着星星男孩，并对他说："快进屋里来，你会在那儿看见你的母亲，她正等着你。"

星星男孩满心欢喜地跑进屋里。然而等他看见等他的人是她时，他便轻蔑地笑起来，说："喂，我母亲在什么地方？我怎么只看见这么个肮脏的讨饭女人。"

女人回答说："我是你的母亲。"

"你是疯了才这么说的，"星星男孩愤愤地大声喊道，"我不是你的儿子，因为你是一个乞丐，而且又丑又穿得破烂。所以你还是快滚吧，不要让我再看见你这张讨厌的脸。"

"不，你的确是我的小儿子呀，你是我在森林中生的。"她大声喊道，说着一下子跪在地上，双手伸向他。"强盗们把你从我身边偷走，又把你扔在林里想让你死，"她喃喃地说，"可是我一看见你，就认出了你，我也认得那些信物：金线织的斗篷和琥珀项链。我求你跟我走吧，为了寻找你，我已经走遍了整个世界。跟我走吧，我的儿，因为我需要你的爱。"

不过星星男孩却丝毫不为所动，铁着心硬生生地拒绝女人的要求，这时除了女人痛苦的哭声外，一点声息也没有。

最后他终于开口了，但声音却生硬而残酷。"假若你真是我的母亲，"他说，"那么你最后还是走得远远的，不要再到这儿来给我丢脸了，因为你知道我以为我是星星的孩子，而不是像你刚才所说的是一个乞丐的孩子。所以你还是离开这儿吧，不要再让我看见你。"

"唉！我的儿子，"她哭着，"在我离开之前你都不愿意吻我一下吗？我经历了多少苦难才找到了你呀。"

"不，"星星男孩说，"你太丑陋了，我宁愿去吻毒蛇，去吻蟾蜍，也不要吻你。"

那女人只得站起身来，伤心地哭泣着走回森林中去

了，星星男孩看见她走了，他很高兴，便跑回到他的同伴那儿，准备去跟他们一块儿玩。

　　可是当他们看见他跑过来时，都纷纷嘲笑他说："你怎么跟蟾蜍一样丑陋，同毒蛇一样可恶呢？你快滚开吧，因为我们不能忍受和你在一起玩。"于是他们把他赶出了花园。

　　星星男孩皱了皱眉头，自言自语地说道："他们为什么会这样说我？我要到水井边去，去那儿看看自己，水井会告诉我，我是多么漂亮。"

　　他来到了水井边，朝井中望去，啊！他的脸就跟蟾蜍一模一样，他的身子也像毒蛇一样长满鳞片。他一下子扑倒在草地上，痛哭起来，自言自语地说："这一定是我的报应。因为我不认我自己的母亲，并赶走了她，对她又傲慢又残酷。我要走遍全世界去寻找她，不找到她决不罢休。"

　　这时樵夫的小女儿朝他走了过来，手扶在他的肩膀上，对他说："你失去了美貌有什么关系？你还是跟我们住在一起吧，我们不会挖苦你的。"

　　他对她说："不，我对待自己的母亲太残忍了，这种惩罚就是对我恶行的报应。所以我得马上走，走遍全世界去寻找我的母亲，直到找到她，得到她对我的宽恕。"

　　所以他朝森林跑去，呼唤着他的母亲，叫她回到自己的身边来，但是却没有一点回应。一整天他都在唤她，太阳下山时，他躺下来在树叶铺成的床上睡觉，鸟儿和野兽见到他也都纷纷逃开了，因为它们仍然记得他的残忍，除了蟾蜍和缓缓爬过的毒蛇，那里就只有他自己一个人。

早晨他爬起身来，从树上摘下几个苦果子充饥，然后穿过大森林朝前走去，一路上伤心地哭着。不论他遇到谁，他都要上前询问，是否看见过他的母亲。

他对鼹鼠说："你能够到地底下去，告诉我，我的母亲在那儿吗？"

鼹鼠却回答说："你已经把我的眼睛弄瞎了。我怎么会知道呢？"

他又对梅花雀说："你可以飞到好高好高的树顶，可以看见整个世界。告诉我，你能看见我的母亲吗？"

梅花雀却回答说："你为了取乐已经剪掉了我的翅膀，我怎么能飞起来呢？"

对那只孤零零住在杉树上的小松鼠，他开口说道："我的母亲在什么地方？"

小松鼠回答说："你已经杀死了我的母亲。难道你也想杀死你的母亲吗？"

星星男孩哭着，低下了头，恳求上帝创造的这些生物们能够宽恕他，然后继续在森林里穿行，寻找那位讨饭的女人。到了第三天他走到了森林的尽头，又来到了平原上。

他走过村子的时候，孩子们都嘲笑他，并朝他扔石头，乡下人甚至连谷仓都不愿让他睡，因为他看上去是那么脏，生怕他会把储存的谷物给弄霉了，就连雇工都赶他走，这里没有一个人怜悯他。他也听不到一点关于他母亲的消息，虽然三年来他走遍了世界各地，甚至常常感到她就在前面的路上走着。他常常呼唤着她，追赶着她，直到他的双脚被尖硬的石块磨出了血来。但是他始终也追不上她，而那些住在路边的人都说他们没有看见过她，或像她那样的女人，他们都拿他的悲痛寻开心。

三年来他走遍了全世界，在这个世界上他既得不到爱，也得不到关心，更得不到仁爱，然而这种世界正是他从前得意的时候为自己制造的呀。

一天傍晚，他来到一处靠河的城门口，那城墙异常坚固。虽然已经非常疲倦，双脚也疼痛难忍，但他还是要进城去。守门的卫兵把刺刀横下来拦住他，粗暴地盘问："你进城干什么？"

"我在寻找我的母亲，"他回答说，"我恳求你准许我进城去，也许她就在这个城里。"

然而卫兵们却挖苦他，他们中的一人捻着胡须，放下手中的盾牌，大声吼道："说实话，你母亲看见你这个样子，她一定不会高兴的，因为你比沼泽地里的蟾蜍和那儿爬行的毒蛇还要令人恶心。快滚开，快滚开，你的母亲没有住在这座城里。"

　　另一个手执黄旗的卫兵对他说："谁是你的母亲，你为什么要找她呢？"

　　他回答说，"我母亲跟我一样也是个乞丐，我从前待她很不好，我恳求你允许我进去吧，若她在城里，找到她，或许她会宽恕我的。"不过他们仍不让他进城，还用长矛去刺他。

　　星星男孩只好哭着转身走了，这时有一个人走了过来，这人身穿镀金铠甲，盔上蹲着飞狮，他询问卫兵是谁要求要进城来。卫兵们回答说："是个要饭的，他的母亲也是个要饭的，我们已经把他给赶走了。"

　　"不要，"那人笑着大声地说，"我们可以把这个丑家伙当奴隶卖掉，说不定可以卖到一碗甜酒的价钱。"

　　旁边正经过一个面目狰狞的老人，他大声说道："我会出个价钱买下他。"等他付了钱后，就拉着星星男孩的手，带着他进城去了。

他们走过好几条街道，来到石榴树遮掩下的一扇小门前。老人用一只刻纹的碧玉戒指在小门上挨了一下，门就打开了，他们走下五级铜阶，来到了一个长满了黑色罂粟花的花园，那里有很多绿色的瓷瓦罐。老人从他的缠头布上取下一条绸纹手帕，用它蒙住星星男孩的眼睛，并赶着星星男孩在他前面走。等到把绸纹手帕从星星男孩双眼上拿开时，星星男孩发现自己在一座地牢中，那儿点着一盏牛角灯。

　　老人在星星男孩面前放上一个木盘，里面装着发了霉的面包，并对他说："吃吧！，"还用一个杯子盛了些污水，又对他说："喝吧！"等星星男孩吃喝完毕，老人便走出去，用铁索拴紧了大门。

　　第二天老人又来见他，这位老人其实是利比亚诸位法师中法术最高超的一位，他的本领是从住在尼罗河坟墓中的一位大师那儿学来的。老人皱着眉头对他说："在这座邪教徒的城门附近有一片森林，林中有三块金币。一块是白金的，一块是黄金的，还有一块是赤金的。今天你要把白金的那块给我拿回来，如果你拿不回来，我就要抽打你一百鞭子。你快快去吧，在太阳落山的时候，我会在花园的门口等你。记住是把白金的拿回来，否则你会倒霉的，因为你是我的奴隶，我花了一碗甜酒的价钱把你买下来的。"他又用那块绸纹手帕蒙住星星男孩的双眼，领着他走出了房子，穿过罂粟花的花园，走上五级铜阶。他用戒指打开了那扇小门以后，把星星男孩放在街上了。

于是星星男孩走出了城门，来到法师告诉他的那片森林。

从外面看去，这片森林真是美丽无比，似乎处处都是鸟语花香的景象。星星男孩兴奋地走了进去。然而森林的美并没有给他带来什么好处，因为不论他要去什么地方，地上都会冒出又粗又尖的荆棘，阻挡住他的去路，凶恶的荨麻会刺他，水飞蓟也用尖刺来扎他，把他搞得疼痛难忍。从早上找到中午，从中午找到日落，星星男孩始终找不到法师所说的白金。日落以后他只好转身，一路哭着回去了，因为他不知道有什么样的命运在等待着他。

可是就在他来到森林边缘时，他听见了林中传来一声痛苦的叫声。他一下子忘记了自己的烦恼，跑回森林，他看见一只小兔子掉进了猎人设下的陷阱里。

星星男孩对它很怜悯，就把它给放了，并对它说："我自己也只是个奴隶，不过，我可以给你自由。"

兔子回答他说："你的确给了我自由，我拿什么来回报你呢？"

星星男孩对它说："我正在寻找一块白金，可我哪儿也找不到它，如果我不能把它找回来给我的主人，他便会打我的。"

"你就跟我来吧，"兔子说，"我会带你去的，因为我知道它藏在什么地方，而且为什么要藏在那儿。"

于是星星男孩跟在兔子身后，啊！就在一棵老橡树的裂缝中，他看见自己要寻找的那块白金。他兴奋得不得了，拿起白金对兔子说："我不过为你做了一点小事，你却加倍地偿还我；我不过对你施了一点小恩，你却百倍地报答我。"

"不是的，"兔子回答说，"你怎样对我，我就怎样对你，仅此而已。"说完兔子就跑开了，星星男孩也回城了。

在城门口坐着一个麻风病人，他的脸上盖着一块绿麻布的头巾，他那双眼睛像烧红的炭，从麻布上的小眼洞里闪着光芒。他看见星星男孩走了过来，便敲击着木碗，并摇着他的铃，呼唤着星星男孩："给我一点钱吧，否则我会饿死的。他们把我赶出了城，谁也不怜悯我。"

"哎呀！"星星男孩大声叹道，"我的钱包里只有一个钱币呀，要是我不把它带给我的主人，他就会打我，因为我是他的奴隶。"

不过麻风病人仍旧缠着他，恳求着他，后来星星男孩终于动了怜悯之心，把白金币给了他。

星星男孩回到法师的房间，法师为他打开门，让他进了屋，问道："你取到那块白金币吗？"星星男孩却回答说："我没有拿到。"于是法师抓住他一顿痛打，随后在他面前放了一个空木盘，对他说："吃吧。"又给了他一个空杯子，说道："喝吧。"然后又把他推到地牢中去了。

第二天法师又来到他身边，对他说："如果你今天不能给我拿回那块黄金币，你就得一辈子做我的奴隶，而且我还要抽打你三百下。"

于是星星男孩又到森林中去了，一整天他都在森林中寻找那块黄金币，可是哪儿也找不到。日落时他便坐下来，开始哭了起来，就在哭的时候，小兔子又跑来了，就是他从陷阱中救出来的那只小兔子。

兔子对他说："你为什么哭了？你又在林中寻找什么呢？"

星星男孩回答说："我在寻找一块黄金币，它就藏在这片林子里，如果我不能把它带回去的话，我的主人就会打我，并把我当奴隶对待。"

"跟我来吧，"兔子大声喊着，它穿过林子，直到跑
到一个水池旁。那块金币就躺在水池的底部。

"我不知如何感谢你？"星星男孩说，"对了，这已经是你第二次救我了。"

"别客气，是你先怜悯我的。"兔子说完，就飞快地跑走了。

星星男孩拿到了那块黄金币，把它放在口袋中，匆匆地朝城里赶去。可是那个麻风病人看见他走过来，就跑上来迎住他，跪倒在他的面前，哭着说，"给我一点钱吧，否则我会给饿死的。"

星星男孩对他说："我口袋里只有一块黄金币，如果我不把它交给我的主人，他会打我，并让我继续当奴隶的。"

然而麻风病人却仍旧苦苦地哀求，于是星星男孩又动了怜悯之心，把这一块黄金币又给了他。

他回到法师的屋中，法师为他开了门，让他进来，对他说："你拿到那块黄金币了吗？"星星男孩便对他说："我没有拿到它，"法师抓住他又痛打一顿，并用链条把他锁上，扔进了地牢里。

第三天法师来到他身边，对他说："如果你今天把那块赤金币给我带回来，我会放了你的，但是你若是带不回来，我肯定会把你杀了。"

　　于是星星男孩又回到了森林中，一整天他都在寻觅那块赤金币，但是哪儿也找不到。到了晚上，他坐下身来，哭泣起来，就在他哭的时候，小兔子来到了他的面前。

　　兔子对他说："你要找的那块赤金币就在你身后的那个山洞里。所以你不用再哭了，你应该高兴才对。"

　　"我如何才能报答你呀，"星星男孩大声说，"啊，这已是你第三次救我了。"

"不用客气，是你先怜悯我的，"兔子说完，就匆匆地跑开了。

星星男孩进入了山洞中，在洞底的角落他发现了那块赤金币。于是他把它放进了口袋，急忙返回城里。那个麻风病人看见他来了，就站在路的中央，高声痛哭起来，并对他说："快给我那块赤金币，否则我一定会死的。"星星男孩又一次怜悯了他，把那块赤金币给了他，说道："你比我更需要它。"然而这时他的心情是沉重的，因为他清楚是什么样的噩运在等待着他。

可是啊！在他经过城门口的时候，卫兵们都向他鞠躬行礼，口中说道："我们的皇上多么漂亮啊！"一群市民跟着他，高声欢呼道："整个世界的确没有比他更漂亮的人了！"星星男孩却哭了起来，同时对自己说："他们又嘲笑我了，拿我的不幸寻开心。"人越聚越多，他在人群中迷了路，最后发现自己来到了一个巨大的广场上，这儿正是国王的宫殿。

王宫的大门打开了，僧侣和大臣们都出来迎接他，他们对他鞠躬行礼，并说："您就是我们正在恭候的皇上，您就是国王的儿子。"

星星男孩回答他们说："我不是国王的儿子，而是一

夜莺与玫瑰

244

个穷要饭的女人的儿子。你们为何说我漂亮？我知道我的长相有多丑。"

这时，身穿镀金铠甲，盔上蹲着飞狮的人拿起盾牌给星星男孩当镜子，大声说道："我的皇上怎么能说他自己不漂亮呢？"

星星男孩举目望去，啊！他自己的脸又跟从前一样了，他的美貌又恢复如前了，而且他还看到自己的眼中有一种以前从未见过的东西。

僧侣和大臣们跪在他面前，对他说："一个古老的预言曾经说过，就在今天有一个人要来统治我们。所以，请我们的皇上接受这顶王冠和这根权杖，用他的公正和仁慈来统治我们吧。"

不过他却对他们说："我不配做一国之君，因为我连自己的生母都不认，而且在没有找到她之前，在没有得到她宽恕之前，我是不会停下的。所以还是让我走吧，因为我要再次走遍世界各地，我是不会留在这儿的，尽管你们要把王冠和权杖给我，也没有用。"说完这番话后，他就转过身去，朝着通向城门的街上走去，看啊，在士兵们周围挤着的一群人中间，他看见了自己那位讨饭的母亲，在她的身旁站着那个麻风病人，他就站在大路中间。

星星男孩

他突然兴奋得叫了起来，立即跑过去，跪下身子，去吻他母亲脚上的伤口，用自己的泪水去洗它们。他把头垂在尘埃中，哭泣着，像一个心碎的人儿，他对她说："母亲，我在自己得意的时候没有认你。如今我失意了，你就收下我吧。母亲，我曾恩将仇报，请把你的爱给我吧。母亲，我拒绝过你，现在就请你收下你的孩子吧。"可是讨饭的女人没有回答他一个字。

　　他又伸出双手，抓住那个麻风病人的一双苍白的脚，对他说："我曾三次怜悯过你。请叫我的母亲对我说一句话。"可是麻风病人也不回答他一个字。

　　他又哭了起来，说："母亲，我的痛苦已经让我忍受不了啦。你就宽恕我吧，让我回到森林中去。"讨饭的女人把手放在他的头上，并对他说："起来吧。"麻风病人也把手放在他的头上，说："起来吧。"

　　他站起身来，望着他们，啊！原来他们正是国王和王后。

　　王后对他说："这是你的父亲，你曾救过他。"

　　国王说："这是你的母亲，你用泪水洗过她的双脚。"

　　他们俯身搂住他的脖子，吻他，并带他回王宫，给他穿上漂亮的衣服，戴上王冠，把权杖放在他的手中，从此他统治着座落于河边的这个城市，成为了它的国王。他对所有的人都表现出了极大的公正和仁慈，他赶走了那个邪恶的法师，并送了好多财宝给樵夫和他的妻子，并把无比的荣誉给了他们的儿女们。他不能容忍任何人虐待鸟兽，且用爱、仁慈和宽恕去教育人民，他把面包送给穷人，把衣服送给赤身裸体的人，在这个王国里充满了和平和繁荣。

然而他的统治时间并不长，因为他受的磨难太深了，遭遇的考验太重了，三年过后，他就去世了。他的后继者却是一个非常坏的统治者。

The Star-Child

Once upon a time two poor Woodcutters were making their way home through a great pine-forest. It was winter, and a night of bitter cold. The snow lay thick upon the ground, and upon the branches of the trees: the frost kept snapping the little twigs on either side of them, as they passed: and when they came to the Mountain-Torrent she was hanging motionless in air, for the Ice-King had kissed her.

So cold was it that even the animals and the birds did not know what to make of it.

"Ugh!" snarled the Wolf as he limped through the brushwood with his tail between his legs, "this is perfectly monstrous weather. Why doesn't the Government look to it?"

"Weet! weet! weet! twittered the green Linnets, "the old Earth is dead, and they have laid her out in her white shroud."

"The Earth is going to be married, and this is her bridal dress," whispered the Turtle-doves to each other. Their little pink feet were quite frost-bitten, but they felt that it was their duty to take a romantic view of the situation.

"Nonsense!" growled the Wolf. "I tell you that it is all the fault of the Government, and if you don't believe me I shall eat you." The Wolf had a thoroughly practical mind, and was never at a loss for a good argument.

"Well, for my own part," said the Woodpecker, who was a born philosopher, "I don't care an atomic theory for explanations. If a thing is so, it is so, and at present it is terribly cold."

Terribly cold it certainly was. The little Squirrels, who lived inside the tall fir-tree, kept rubbing each other's noses to keep themselves warm, and the Rabbits curled themselves up in their holes, and did not venture even to look out of doors. The only people who seemed to enjoy it were the great

星星男孩

horned Owls. Their feathers were quite stiff with rime, but they did not mind, and they rolled their large yellow eyes, and called out to each other across the forest, "Tu-whit! Tu-whoo![1] Tu-whit! Tu-whoo! What delightful weather we are having!"

On and on went the two Woodcutters, blowing lustily upon their fingers, and stamping with their huge iron-shod boots upon the caked snow. Once they sank into a deep drift, and came out as white as millers are, when the stones are grinding; and once they slipped on the hard smooth ice where the marsh-water was frozen, and their faggots fell out of their bundles, and they had to pick them up and bind them together again; and once they thought that they had lost their way, and a great terror seized on them, for they knew that the Snow is cruel to those who sleep in her arms. But they put their trust in the good Saint Martin, who watches over all travellers, and retraced their steps, and went warily,

---

[1] tu-whit, tu-whoo 均为拟声词，指猫头鹰的叫声。

and at last they reached the outskirts of the forest, and saw, far down in the valley beneath them, the lights of the village in which they dwelt.

So overjoyed were they at their deliverance that they laughed aloud, and the Earth seemed to them like a flower of silver, and the Moon like a flower of gold.

Yet, after they had laughed they became sad, for they remembered their poverty, and one of them said to the other, "Why did we make merry, seeing that life is for the rich, and not for such as we are? Better that we had died of cold in the forest, or that some wild beast had fallen upon us and slain us."

"Truly," answered his companion," much is given to some, and little is given to others. Injustice has parcelled out the world, nor is there equal division of aught save of sorrow."

But as they were bewailing their misery to each other this strange thing happened. There fell from

星星男孩

heaven a very bright and beautiful star. It slipped down the side of the sky, passing by the other stars in its course, and, as they watched it wondering, it seemed to them to sink behind a clump of willow-trees that stood hard by a little sheep-fold no more than a stone's throw away.

"Why! There is a crock of gold for whoever finds it," they cried, and they set to and ran, so eager were they for the gold.

And one of them ran faster than his mate, and outstripped him, and forced his way through the willows, and came out on the other side, and lo! there was indeed a thing of gold lying on the white snow. So he hastened towards it, and stooping down placed his hands upon it, and it was a cloak of golden tissue, curiously wrought with stars, and wrapped in many folds. And he cried out to his comrade that he had found the treasure that had fallen from the sky, and when his comrade had come up, they sat them down in the snow, and

夜莺与玫瑰

loosened the folds of the cloak that they might divide the pieces of gold. But, alas! no gold was in it, nor silver, nor, indeed, treasure of any kind, but only a little child who was asleep.

And one of them said to the other: "This is a bitter ending to our hope, nor have we any good fortune, for what doth❶ a child profit to a man? Let us leave it here, and go our way, seeing that we are poor men, and have children of our own whose bread we may not give to another."

But his companion answered him: "Nay, but it were an evil thing to leave the child to perish here in the snow, and though I am as poor as thou art, and have many mouths to feed, and but little in the pot, yet will I bring it home with me, and my wife shall have care of it."

So very tenderly he took up the child, and wrapped the cloak around it to shield it from the harsh cold, and made his way down the hill to

星
星
男
孩

❶ doth 　（古英语）do的第三人称单数。

the village, his comrade marvelling much at his foolishness and softness of heart.

And when they came to the village, his comrade said to him, "Thou hast[1] the child, therefore give me the cloak, for it is meet that we should share."

But he answered him: "Nay, for the cloak is neither mine nor thine, but the child's only," and he bade him Godspeed[2], and went to his own house and knocked.

And when his wife opened the door and saw that her husband had returned safe to her, she put her arms round his neck and kissed him, and took from his back the bundle of faggots, and brushed the snow off his boots, and bade him come in.

But he said to her, "I have found something in the forest, and I have brought it to thee to have care of it," and he stirred not from the threshold.

"What is it?" she cried. "Show it to me, for the house is bare, and we have need of many things."

---

❶ hast （古英语）同have。
❷ Godspeed　旧时用法，相当于Good luck，对即将启程的人的祝福语。

And he drew the cloak back, and showed her the sleeping child.

"Alack[1], goodman!" she murmured, "have we not children enough of our own, that thou must needs bring a changeling to sit by the hearth? And who knows if it will not bring us bad fortune? And how shall we tend it?" And she was wroth against him.

"Nay, but it is a Star-Child," he answered; and he told her the strange manner of the finding of it.

But she would not be appeased, but mocked him, and spoke angrily, and cried: "Our children lack bread, and shall we feed the child of another? Who is there who careth[2] for us? And who giveth[3] us food?"

"Nay, but God careth for the sparrows even, and feedeth[4] them," he answered.

"Do not the sparrows die of hunger in the winter?" she asked. "And is it not winter now? "And the man answered nothing, but stirred not from the threshold.

---

[1] alack （古英语） 啊呀。
[2] careth （古英语）同 care。
[3] giveth （古英语）同 give。
[4] feedeth （古英语）同 feed。

And a bitter wind from the forest came in through the open door, and made her tremble, and she shivered, and said to him: "Wilt thou not close the door? There cometh a bitter wind into the house, and I am cold."

"Into a house where a heart is hard cometh there not always a bitter wind?" he asked. And the woman answered him nothing, but crept closer to the fire.

And after a time she turned round and looked at him, and her eyes were full of tears. And he came in swiftly, and placed the child in her arms, and she kissed it, and laid it in a little bed where the youngest of their own children was lying.

And on the morrow the Woodcutter took the curious cloak of gold and placed it in a great chest, and a chain of amber that was round the child's neck his wife took and set it in the chest also.

So the Star-Child was brought up with the children of the Woodcutter, and sat at the same board with them, and was their playmate. And every year he became more beautiful to look at, so that all those who dwelt in the village were filled with wonder, for, while they were swarthy and black-haired, he was white and delicate as sawn ivory, and his curls were like the rings of the daffodil. His lips, also, were like the petals of a red flower, and his eyes were like violets by a river of pure water, and his body like the narcissus of a field where the mower comes not.

Yet did his beauty work him evil. For he grew proud, and cruel, and selfish. The children of the Woodcutter, and the other children of the village, he despised, saying that they were of mean parentage, while he was noble, being sprang from a Star, and he made himself master over them, and called them his servants. No pity had he for the poor, or for those who were blind or maimed or in any way afflicted, but would cast stones at them and drive them forth on to the highway, and bid them beg their bread

星星男孩

elsewhere, so that none save the outlaws came twice to that village to ask for aims. Indeed, he was as one enamoured of beauty, and would mock at the weakly and ill-favoured, and make jest of them; and himself he loved, and in summer, when the winds were still, he would lie by the well in the priest's orchard and look down at the marvel of his own face, and laugh for the pleasure he had in his fairness.

Often did the Woodcutter and his wife chide him, and say: "We did not deal with thee as thou dealest with those who are left desolate, and have none to succour them. Wherefore art thou so cruel to all who need pity?"

Often did the old priest send for him, and seek to teach him the love of living things, saying to him: "The fly is thy brother. Do it no harm. The wild birds that roam through the forest have their freedom. Snare them not for thy pleasure. God made the blind-worm and the mole, and each has its place.

Who art thou to bring pain into God's world? Even the cattle of the field praise Him."

But the Star-Child heeded not their words, but would frown and flout, and go back to his companions, and lead them. And his companions followed him, for he was fair, and fleet of foot, and could dance, and pipe, and make music. And wherever the Star-Child led them they followed, and whatever the Star-Child bade them do, that did they. And when he pierced with a sharp reed the dim eyes of the mole, they laughed, and when he cast stones at the leper they laughed also. And in all things he ruled them, and they became hard of heart, even as he was.

Now there passed one day through the village a poor beggar-woman. Her garments were torn and ragged, and her feet were bleeding from the rough road on which she had travelled, and she was in very evil plight. And being weary she sat her down under a chestnut-tree to rest.

星星男孩

But when the Star-Child saw her, he said to his companions, "See! There sitteth[1] a foul beggar-woman under that fair and green-leaved tree. Come, let us drive her hence, for she is ugly and ill-favoured."

So he came near and threw stones at her, and mocked her, and she looked at him with terror in her eyes, nor did she move her gaze from him. And when the Woodcutter, who was cleaving logs in a haggard hard by, saw what the Star-Child was doing, he ran up and rebuked him, and said to him: "Surely thou art hard of heart and knowest not mercy, for what evil has this poor woman done to thee that thou shouldst treat her in this wise?"

And the Star-Child grew red with anger, and stamped his foot upon the ground, and said, "Who art thou to question me what I do? I am no son of thine to do thy bidding."

夜莺与玫瑰

---

[1] sitteth （古英语）同 sit。

"Thou speakest[1] truly," answered the Woodcutter, "yet did I show thee pity when I found thee in the forest."

And when the woman heard these words she gave a loud cry, and fell into a swoon. And the Woodcutter carried her to his own house, and his wife had care of her, and when she rose up from the swoon into which she had fallen, they set meat and drink before her, and bade her have comfort.

But she would neither eat nor drink, but said to the Woodcutter, "Didst[2] thou not say that the child was found in the forest? And was it not ten years from this day?"

And the Woodcutter answered, "Yea, it was in the forest that I found him, and it is ten years from this day."

"And what signs didst thou find with him?" she cried. "Bare he not upon his neck a chain of amber?

星
星
男
孩

---

❶ speakest　（古英语）同speak。

❷ didst　（古英语）同did。

Was not round him a cloak of gold tissue broidered with stars?"

"Truly," answered the Woodcutter, "it was even as thou sayest." And he took the cloak and the amber chain from the chest where they lay, and showed them to her.

And when she saw them she wept for joy, and said, "He is my little son whom I lost in the forest. I pray thee send for him quickly, for in search of him have I wandered over the whole world."

So the Woodcutter and his wife went out and called to the Star-Child, and said to him, "Go into the house, and there shalt thou find thy mother, who is waiting for thee."

So he ran in, filled with wonder and great gladness. But when he saw her who was waiting there, he laughed scornfully and said, "Why, where is my mother? For I see none here but this vile beggar-woman."

And the woman answered him, "I am thy mother."

"Thou art mad to say so," cried the Star-Child angrily. "I am no son of thine, for thou art a beggar, and ugly, and in rags. Therefore get thee hence, and let me see thy foul face no more."

"Nay, but thou art indeed my little son, whom I bare in the forest," she cried, and she fell on her knees, and held out her arms to him. "The robbers stole thee from me, and left thee to die," she murmured, "but I recognized thee when I saw thee, and the signs also have I recognized, the cloak of golden tissue and the amber-chain. Therefore I pray thee come with me, for over the whole world have I wandered in search of thee. Come with me, my son, for I have need of thy love."

But the Star-Child stirred not from his place, but shut the doors of his heart against her, nor was there any sound heard save the sound of the woman weeping for pain.

And at last he spoke to her, and his voice was hard and bitter. "If in very truth thou art my mother,"

星
星
男
孩

he said, "it had been better hadst thou stayed away, and not come here to bring me to shame, seeing that I thought I was the child of some Star and not a beggar's child, as thou tellest❶ me that I am. Therefore get thee hence, and let me see thee no more."

"Alas! my son," she cried, "wilt thou not kiss me before I go? For I have suffered much to find thee."

"Nay," said the Star-Child, "but thou art too foul to look at and rather would I kiss the adder or the toad than thee."

So the woman rose up, and went away into the forest weeping bitterly, and when the Star-Child saw that she had gone, he was glad, and ran back to his playmates that he might play with them.

But when they beheld him coming, they mocked him and said, "Why, thou art as foul as the toad, and

❶ tellest （古英语） 同tell。

as loathsome as the adder. Get thee hence, for we will not suffer thee to play with us," and they drave[1] him out of the garden.

And the Star-Child frowned and said to himself, "What is this that they say to me? I will go to the well of water and look into it, and it shall tell me of my beauty."

So he went to the well of water and looked into it, and lo! his face was as the face of a toad, and his body was sealed like an adder. And he flung himself down on the grass and wept, and said to himself, "Surely this has come upon me by reason of my sin. For I have denied my mother, and driven her away, and been proud, and cruel to her. Wherefore I will go and seek her through the whole world, nor will I rest till I have found her."

And there came to him the little daughter of the Woodcutter, and she put her hand upon his

---

[1] drave （古英语）drive的过去式。

星星男孩

shoulder and said, "What doth it matter if thou hast lost thy comeliness? Stay with us, and I will not mock at thee."

And he said to her, "Nay, but I have been cruel to my mother, and as a punishment has this evil been sent to me. Wherefore I must go hence, and wander through the world till I find her, and she give me her forgiveness."

So he ran away into the forest and called out to his mother to come to him, but there was no answer. All day long he called to her, and when the sun set he lay down to sleep on a bed of leaves, and the birds and the animals fled from him, as they remembered his cruelty, and he was alone save for the toad that watched him, and the slow adder that crawled past.

And in the morning he rose up, and plucked some bitter berries from the trees and ate them, and took his way through the great wood, weeping sorely. And of everything that he met he made enquiry if

夜
莺
与
玫
瑰

perchance they had seen his mother.

He said to the Mole, "Thou canst go beneath the earth. Tell me, is my mother there?"

And the Mole answered, "Thou hast blinded mine eyes. How should I know?"

He said to the Linnet, "Thou canst fly over the tops of the tall trees, and canst see the whole world. Tell me, canst thou see my mother?"

And the Linnet answered, "Thou hast clipt❶ my wings for thy pleasure. How should I fly?"

And to the little Squirrel who lived in the fir-tree, and was lonely, he said, "Where is my mother?"

And the Squirrel answered, "Thou hast slain mine. Dost thou seek to slay thine also?"

And the Star-Child wept and bowed his head, and prayed forgiveness of God's things, and went on through the forest, seeking for the beggar-woman. And on the third day he came to the other side of

---

❶ clipt （古英语） clip的过去式。

the forest and went down into the plain.

And when he passed through the villages the children mocked him, and threw stones at him, and the carlots would not suffer him even to sleep in the byres lest he might bring mildew on the stored corn, so foul was he to look at, and their hired men drave him away, and there was none who had pity on him. Nor could he hear anywhere of the beggar-woman who was his mother, though for the space of three years he wandered over the world, and often seemed to see her on the road in front of him, and would call to her, and run after her till the sharp flints made his feet to bleed. But overtake her he could not, and those who dwelt by the way did ever deny that they had seen her, or any like to her, and they made sport of his sorrow.

For the space of three years he wandered over the world, and in the world there was neither love nor loving-kindness nor charity for him, but it was

夜
莺
与
玫
瑰

even such a world as he had made for himself in the days of his great pride.

And one evening he came to the gate of a strong-walled city that stood by a river, and, weary and footsore though he was, he made to enter in. But the soldiers who stood on guard dropped their halberts across the entrance, and said roughly to him, "What is thy business in the city?"

"I am seeking for my mother," he answered, "and I pray ye to suffer me to pass, for it may be that she is in this city."

But they mocked at him, and one of them wagged a black beard, and set down his shield and cried, "Of a truth, thy mother will not be merry when she sees thee, for thou art more ill-favoured than the toad of the marsh, or the adder that crawls in the fen. Get thee gone. Get thee gone. Thy mother dwells not in this city."

And another, who held a yellow banner in his hand, said to him, "Who is thy mother, and

星星男孩

wherefore art thou seeking for her?"

And he answered, "My mother is a beggar even as I am, and I have treated her evilly, and I pray ye to suffer me to pass that she may give me her forgiveness, if it be that she tarrieth❶ in this city." But they would not, and pricked him with their spears.

And, as he turned away weeping, one whose armour was inlaid with gilt flowers, and on whose helmet couched a lion that had wings, came up and made enquiry of the soldiers who it was who had sought entrance. And they said to him, "It is a beggar and the child of a beggar, and we have driven him away."

"Nay," he cried, laughing, "but we will sell the foul thing for a slave, and his price shall be the price of a bowl of sweet wine."

And an old and evil-visaged man who was passing by called out, and said, "I will buy him for

---

❶ tarrieth （古英语） 同tarry。

that price," and, when he had paid the price, he took the Star—Child by the hand and led him into the city.

And after that they had gone through many streets they came to a little door that was set in a wall that was covered with a pomegranate tree. And the old man touched the door with a ring of graved jasper and it opened, and they went down five steps of brass into a garden filled with black poppies and green jars of burnt clay. And the old man took then from his turban a scarf of figured silk, and bound with it the eyes of the Star—Child, and drave him in front of him. And when the scarf was taken off his eyes, the Star—Child found himself in a dungeon, that was lit by a lantern of horn.

And the old man set before him some mouldy bread on a trencher and said, "Eat," and some brackish water in a cup and said, "Drink," and when he had eaten and drunk, the old man went out, locking the door behind

星星男孩

him and fastening it with an iron chain.

And on the morrow the old man, who was indeed the subtlest[1] of the magicians of Libya and had learned his art from one who dwelt in the tombs of the Nile, came in to him and frowned at him, and said, "In a wood that is nigh to the gate of this city of Giaours there are three pieces of gold. One is of white gold, and another is of yellow gold, and the gold of the third one is red. Today thou shalt bring me the piece of white gold, and if thou bringest[2] it not back, I will beat thee with a hundred stripes. Get thee away quickly, and at sunset I will be waiting for thee at the door of the garden. See that thou bringest the white gold, or it shall go in with thee, for thou art my slave, and I have bought thee for the price of a bowl of sweet wine." And he bound the eyes of the Star-Child with the

[1] subtlest （古英语）同subtle。
[2] bringest （古英语）同bring。

scarf of figured silk, and led him through the house, and through the garden of poppies, and up the five steps of brass. And having opened the little door with his ring he set him in the street.

And the Star-Child went out of the gate of the city, and came to the wood of which the Magician had spoken to him.

Now this wood was very fair to look at from without, and seemed full of singing birds and of sweet-scented flowers, and the Star-Child entered it gladly. Yet did its beauty profit him little, for wherever he went harsh briars and thorns shot up from the ground and encompassed him, and evil nettles stung him, and the thistle pierced him with her daggers, so that he was in sore distress. Nor could he anywhere find the piece of white gold of which the Magician had spoken, though he sought for it from morn to noon, and from noon to sunset. And at sunset he set his face towards home,

星星男孩

weeping bitterly, for he knew what fate was in store
for him.

But when he had reached the outskirts of the
wood, he heard from a thicket a cry as of someone
in pain. And forgetting his own sorrow he ran back to
the place, and saw there a little Hare caught in a trap
that some hunter had set for it.

And the Star-Child had pity on it, and released
it, and said to it, "I am myself but a slave, yet may I
give thee thy freedom."

And the Hare answered him, and said: "Surely
thou hast given me freedom, and what shall I give
thee in return?"

And the Star-Child said to it, "I am seeking for a
piece of white gold, nor can I anywhere find it, and if
I bring it not to my master he will beat me."

"Come thou with me," said the Hare, "and I will
lead thee to it, for I know where it is hidden, and for
what purpose."

So the Star-Child went with the Hare, and

lo! in the cleft of a great oak-tree he saw the piece of white gold that he was seeking. And he was filled with joy, and seized it, and said to the Hare, "The service that I did to thee thou hast rendered back again many times over and the kindness that I showed thee thou hast repaid a hundred-fold."

"Nay," answered the Hare, "but as thou dealt with me, so I did deal with thee," and it ran away swiftly, and the Star-Child went towards the city.

Now at the gate of the city there was seated one who was a leper. Over his face hung a cowl of grey linen, and through the eyelets his eyes gleamed like red coals. And when he saw the Star-Child coming, he struck upon a wooden bowl, and clattered his bell, and called out to him, and said, "Give me a piece of money, or I must die of hunger. For they have thrust me out of the city, and there is no one who has pity on rite."

"Alas!" cried the Star-Child, "I have but one piece

星星男孩

275

of money in my wallet, and if I bring it not to my master he will beat me for I am his slave."

But the leper entreated him, and prayed of him, till the Star-Child had pity, and gave him the piece of white gold.

And when he came to the Magician's house, the Magician opened to him, and brought him in, and said to him, "Hast thou the piece of white gold?" And the Star-Child answered, "I have it not." So the Magician fell upon him, and beat him, and set before him an empty trencher, and said "Eat," and an empty cup, and said, "Drink," and flung him again into the dungeon.

And on the morrow the Magician came to him, and said, "If today thou bringest me not the piece of yellow gold, I will surely keep thee as my slave, and give thee three hundred stripes."

So the Star-Child went to the wood, and all day long he searched for the piece of yellow gold, but nowhere could he find it. And at sunset he sat him

夜
莺
与
玫
瑰

276

down and began to weep, and as he was weeping there came to him the little Hare that he had rescued from the trap.

And the Hare said to him, "Why art thou weeping? And what dost thou seek in the wood?"

And the Star-Child answered, "I am seeking for a piece of yellow gold that is hidden here, and if I find it not my master will beat me, and keep me as a slave."

"Follow me," cried the Hare, and it ran through the wood till it came to a pool of water. And at the bottom of the pool the piece of yellow gold was lying.

"How shall I thank thee?" said the Star-Child, "for lo! this is the second time that you have succoured me."

"Nay, but thou hadst pity on me first," said the Hare, and it ran away swiftly.

And the Star-Child took the piece of yellow gold, and put it in his wallet, and hurried to the city. But the leper saw him coming, and ran to meet him and

星星男孩

knelt down and cried, "Give me a piece of money or I shall die of hunger."

And the Star-Child said to him, "I have in my wallet but one piece of yellow gold, and if I bring it not to my master he will beat me and keep me as his slave."

But the leper entreated him sore, so that the Star-Child had pity on him, and gave him the piece of yellow gold.

And when he came to the Magician's house, the Magician opened to him, and brought him in, and said to him, "Hast thou the piece of yellow gold?" And the Star-Child said to him, "I have it not." So the Magician fell upon him, and beat him, and loaded him with chains, and cast him again into the dungeon.

And on the morrow the Magician came to him, and said, "If today thou bringest me the piece of red gold I will set thee free, but if thou bringest it not I will surely slay thee."

So the Star-Child went to the wood, and all day long he searched for the piece of red gold, but nowhere could he find it. And at evening he sat him down, and wept, and as he was weeping there came to him the little Hare.

And the Hare said to him, "The piece of red gold that thou seekest is in the cavern that is behind thee. Therefore weep no more but be glad."

"How shall I reward thee," cried the Star-Child, "for lo! this is the third time thou hast succoured me."

"Nay, but thou hadst pity on me first," said the Hare, and it ran away swiftly.

And the Star-Child entered the cavern, and in its farthest corner he found the piece of red gold. So he put it in his wallet, and hurried to the city. And the leper seeing him coming, stood in the centre of the road, and cried out, and said to him, "Give me the piece of red money, or I must die," and the Star-Child had pity on him again, and gave him the piece

星星男孩

279

of red gold, saying, "Thy need is greater than mine."
Yet was his heart heavy, for he knew what evil fate
awaited him.

But lo! as he passed through the gate of the
city, the guards bowed down and made obeisance
to him, saying, "How beautiful is our lord!" and
a crowd of citizens followed him, and cried out,
"Surely there is none so beautiful in the whole
world!" so that the Star-Child wept, and said to
himself, "They are mocking me, and making light
of my misery." And so large was the concourse of
the people, that he lost the threads of his way, and
found himself at last in a great square, in which
there was a palace of a King.

And the gate of the palace opened, and the
priests and the high officers of the city ran forth to
meet him, and they abased themselves before him,
and said, "Thou art our lord for whom we have been
waiting, and the son of our King."

And the Star-Child answered them and said, "I

am no king's son, but the child of a poor beggar-woman. And how say ye that I am beautiful, for I know that I am evil to look at?"

Then he, whose armour was inlaid with gilt flowers, and on whose helmet crouched a lion that had wings, held up a shield, and cried, "How saith[0] my lord that he is not beautiful?"

And the Star-Child looked, and lo! his face was even as it had been, and his comeliness had come back to him, and he saw that in his eyes which he had not seen there before.

And the priests and the high officers knelt down and said to him, "It was prophesied of old that on this day should come he who was to rule over us. Therefore, let our lord take this crown and this sceptre, and be in his justice and mercy our King over us."

But he said to them, "I am not worthy, for

---

❶ saith （古英语）say的第三人称单数。

I have denied the mother who bare me, nor may I rest till I have found her, and known her forgiveness. Therefore, let me go, for I must wander again over the world, and may not tarry here, though ye bring me the crown and the sceptre." And as he spake he turned his face from them towards the street that led to the gate of the city, and lo! amongst the crowd that pressed round the soldiers, he saw the beggar-woman who was his mother, and at her side stood the leper, who had sat by the road.

And a cry of joy broke from his lips, and he ran over, and kneeling down he kissed the wounds on his mother's feet, and wet them with his tears. He bowed his head in the dust, and sobbing, as one whose heart might break, he said to her: "Mother, I denied thee in the hour of my pride. Accept me in the hour of my humility. Mother, I gave thee hatred. Do thou give me love. Mother, I rejected thee. Receive thy child now." But the beggar-woman answered him not a word.

And he reached out his hands, and clasped the white feet of the leper, and said to him: "Thrice did I give thee of my mercy. Bid my mother speak to me once." But the leper answered him not a word.

And he sobbed again, and said: "Mother, my suffering is greater than I can bear. Give me thy forgiveness, and let me go back to the forest." And the beggar-woman put her hand on his head, and said to him, "Rise," and the leper put his hand on his head, and said to him "Rise," also.

And he rose up from his feet, and looked at them, and lo! they were a King and a Queen.

And the Queen said to him, "This is thy father whom thou hast succoured."

And the King said, "This is thy mother, whose feet thou hast washed with thy tears."

And they fell on his neck and kissed him, and brought him into the palace, and clothed him in fair

星星男孩

raiment, and set the crown upon his head, and the sceptre in his hand, and over the city that stood by the river he ruled, and was its lord. Much justice and mercy did he show to all, and the evil Magician he banished, and to the Woodcutter and his wife he sent many rich gifts, and to their children he gave high honour. Nor would he suffer any to be cruel to bird or beast, but taught love and loving-kindness and charity, and to the poor he gave bread, and to the naked he gave raiment, and there was peace and plenty in the land.

Yet ruled he not long, so great had been his suffering, and so bitter the fire of his testing, for after the space of three years he died. And he who came after him ruled evilly.

夜
莺
与
玫
瑰

自私的巨人

每天下午放学后，孩子们总喜欢到巨人的花园里去玩耍。

这是一个很可爱的大花园，长满了绿茸茸的青草，美丽的鲜花随处可见，多得像天上的星星。草地上还长着十二棵桃树，春天开出粉扑扑的团团花朵，秋天里则结下累累果实。栖息在树枝上鸟儿唱着欢乐的曲子，每当这时，嬉戏中的孩子们会停下来侧耳聆听鸟儿的鸣唱，并相互高声喊着："我们多么快乐啊！"

一天，巨人回来了。原来他到自己的妖怪朋友科尼西家串门去了，在妖怪家里一住就是七年。七年的时间里他把要讲的话都讲完了，便决定回家。进了家门，他一眼就看见在花园中戏耍的孩子们。

"你们在这儿干什么？"他粗声粗气地吼叫起来，孩子们都被他吓跑了。

"我的花园就是我的花园，"巨人说，"谁都清楚，除

了我自己，谁也不准来这里玩。"于是，他筑起一堵高高的围墙把花园围起来，还挂出一块告示：

闲人莫入　违者重罚

　　他的确是一个非常自私的巨人。

　　从此可怜的孩子们没有了玩耍的地方，他们只得来到大街上，但是大街上满是尘土和硬硬的石块，让他们扫兴极了。放学后他们仍常常在高耸的围墙外徘徊，谈论着墙内花园中的美丽景色。"从前，在里面我们多么快乐啊。"他们彼此诉说着。

　　春天又来了，整个乡村到处开放着小花，处处有小鸟在欢唱。然而只有自私的巨人的花园却依旧是一片寒冬景象。由于看不见孩子们，小鸟便无心唱歌，树儿也忘了开花。有一朵花儿从草中探出头来，看见那块告示后，它对孩子们的遭遇深感同情，于是又把头缩回去，继续睡觉了。只有雪和霜对此乐不可支。"春天已忘记了这座花园，"他们叫喊着，"这样我们可以一年四季住在这儿了。"雪用她那巨大的白色斗篷把草地遮得严严实实，霜也把所有的树木一齐镀成银色，随后他们还邀请北风和他们同住。北风应邀而至，穿一身毛皮大衣，他整天对

着花园呼啸,把烟囱都刮倒了。"这是个令人开心的地方,"
他说,"我们还得把冰雹叫来。"于是,冰雹来了。每天
三个钟头他不停地敲打着城堡的房顶,把房上的石板砸
得七零八落,然后又围着花园一圈接一圈地猛跑起来。
他浑身上下灰蒙蒙的,呼出阵阵袭人的寒气。

　　"我真弄不懂,春天为什么迟迟不来,"巨人坐在窗
前望着外面冰天雪地的花园说,"我盼望天气发生变化。"

　　然而春天再也没有出现,夏天也不见踪影。秋天把
金色的硕果送给了千家万户的花园,却什么也没给巨人

　　的花园。"他太自私了。"秋天说。就这样，巨人的花园里是终年的寒冬，只有北风、冰雹，还有霜和雪在园中的林间上蹿下跳。

　　一日清晨，巨人睁着双眼躺在床上，这时耳边传来阵阵美妙的音乐。音乐悦耳动听，他想一定是国王的乐师路经此地。原来窗外唱歌的不过是一只小红雀，只因巨人好长时间没听到鸟儿在花园中歌唱，此刻感到它妙不可言。这时，巨人头顶上的冰雹已不再狂舞，北风也停止了呼啸，缕缕芳香透过敞开的窗户扑面而来。"我相信春天终于来到了。"巨人说着，从床上跳起来，朝窗外望去。

　　他看见了什么呢？

他看见了一幕动人的景象：孩子们爬过墙上的小洞已进了花园，正坐在树枝上，每棵树上都坐着一个孩子。迎来了孩子的树木欣喜若狂，并用鲜花把自己打扮一新，还挥动手臂轻轻抚摸孩子们的头。鸟儿们在树梢翩翩起舞，兴奋地欢唱着，花朵也纷纷从草地里伸出头来露着笑脸。这的确是一幅动人的画面。满园春色中只有一个角落仍笼罩在严冬之中，那是花园中最远的一个角落，一个小男孩正孤零零地站在那儿，因为他个头太小爬不上树，只能围着树转来转去，哭泣着不知所措。那棵可怜的树仍被霜雪裹得严严实实的，北风也对它肆意地咆哮着。"快爬上来呀，小孩子！"树说，并尽可能地垂下枝条，可是小孩还是太矮小了。

　　此情此景深深地感化了巨人的心。"我真是太自私了！"他说，"现在我明白为什么春天不肯到我这儿来了。我要把那可怜的孩子抱上树，然后再把围墙都推倒，让我的花园永远成为孩子们的游戏场所。"他真为自己过去的所作所为感到羞愧。

　　巨人轻轻地走下楼，悄悄地打开前门，走到花园里。但是孩子们一看巨人，都吓得逃走了，花园再次回到了冬天里。唯有那个小男孩没有跑，因为他的眼里充满了泪水，没有看见走过来的巨人。巨人悄悄来到小孩的身后，双手轻轻托起孩子放在树枝上。树儿立即怒放出朵朵鲜花，鸟儿们也飞回枝头放声欢唱，小男孩伸出双臂搂着巨人的脖子，亲吻巨人的脸。其他孩子看见巨人不再那么凶恶，都纷纷跑了回来，春天也跟着孩子们来了。"孩子们，这是你们的花园了。"巨人说。接着他提起一把大斧头，把围墙统统给推倒了。中午十二点，人们去赶集的时候，欣喜地看见巨人和孩子们一起在他们所见到的最美丽的花园中游戏玩耍。

自
私
的
巨
人

他们玩了整整一天，夜幕降临后，孩子们向巨人道晚安。

"可你们的那个小伙伴在哪儿呢？"巨人问，"就是我抱到树上的男孩。"巨人最爱那个男孩，因为男孩吻过他。

"我们不知道啊，"孩子们回答说，"他已经走了。"

巨人又说："你们一定要告诉他，叫他明天来这里。"但是孩子们告诉巨人他们不知道小男孩家住何处，而且从前没见过他，巨人听后心里很不是滋味。

每天下午，孩子们一放学就来找巨人一起玩。可是巨人最喜爱的那个小男孩再也没有来过。巨人对每一个小孩都非常友善，然而他更想念那个小男孩，还常常提起他。"我多么想见到他啊！"巨人常常感叹。

许多年过去了，巨人变得年迈而体弱。他已无力再与孩子们一起嬉戏，只能坐在一把巨大的扶手椅上，一边观看孩子们玩游戏，一边欣赏着自己的花园。"我有好多美丽的鲜花，"他说，"但孩子们才是最美的花朵。"

一个冬天的早晨，巨人起床穿衣时朝窗外望了望。现在他已不讨厌冬天了，因为他心里明白这只不过是让春天打个盹，让花儿们歇口气罢了。

突然，他惊讶地揉揉眼，定睛看了又看。眼前的景色真是美妙无比：在花园尽头的角落里，有一棵树上开满了逗人喜爱的白花，满树的枝条金光闪闪，枝头上垂挂着银色的果实，树的下边就站着巨人特别喜爱的那个小男孩。

巨人激动地跑下楼，出门朝花园奔去。他急匆匆地跑过草地，奔向孩子。来到孩子面前，他脸红脖子粗地愤愤说道："谁敢把你弄成这样？"只见孩子的一双小手掌心上留有两个钉痕，他的一双小脚上也有两个钉痕。

"谁敢把你弄成这样？"巨人吼道，"告诉我，我去取我的长剑把他杀死。"

"不要！"孩子回答说，"这些都是爱的烙印啊。"

"你是谁？"巨人说着，心中油然生出一种奇特的敬畏之情。他一下子跪在小男孩的面前。

小男孩面带笑容地看着巨人说道："你让我在你的花园中玩过一次。今天我要带你去我的花园，那就是天堂。"

那天下午孩子们跑进花园的时候，他们看见巨人躺在那棵树下，已经死了，满身都盖着白花。

自
私
的
巨
人

The Selfish Giant

Every afternoon, as they were coming from school, the children used to go and play in the Giant's garden.

It was a large lovely garden, with soft green grass. Here and there over the grass stood beautiful flowers like stars, and there were twelve peach-trees that in the spring-time broke out into delicate blossoms of pink and pearl, and in the autumn bore rich fruit. The birds sat on the trees and sang so sweetly that the children used to stop their games in order to listen to them. "How happy we are here!" they cried to each other.

One day the Giant came back. He had been to visit his friend the Cornish ogre, and had stayed with him for seven years. After the seven years were over he had said all that he had to say, for his conversation was limited, and he determined to return to his own castle. When he arrived he saw the children playing in the garden.

夜莺与玫瑰

298

"What are you doing here?" he cried in a very gruff voice, and the children ran away.

"My own garden is my own garden," said the Giant; "any one can understand that, and I will allow nobody to play in it but myself." So he built a high wall all round it, and put up a notice-board.

TRESPASSERS WILL BE PROSECUTED

He was a very selfish Giant.

The poor children had now nowhere to play. They tried to play on the road, but the road was very dusty and full of hard stones, and they did not like it. They used to wander round the high wall when their lessons were over, and talk about the beautiful garden inside. "How happy we were there," they said to each other.

Then the Spring came, and all over the country there were little blossoms and little birds. Only in the garden of the Selfish Giant it was still winter. The birds did not care to sing in it as there were no children, and the trees forgot to blossom. Once a beautiful flower put its head out from the grass, but when it saw the notice-

自
私
的
巨
人

board it was so sorry for the children that it slipped
back into the ground again, and went off to sleep. The
only people who were pleased were the Snow and the
Frost. "Spring has forgotten this garden," they cried, "so
we will live here all the year round." The Snow covered
up the grass with her great white cloak, and the Frost
painted all the trees silver. Then they invited the North
Wind to stay with them, and he came. He was wrapped
in furs, and he roared all day about the garden, and blew
the chimney-pots down. "This is a delightful spot," he
said, "we must ask the Hail on a visit." So the Hail came.
Every day for three hours he rattled on the roof of the
castle till he broke most of the slates, and then he ran
round and round the garden as fast as he could go. He
was dressed in grey, and his breath was like ice.

"I cannot understand why the Spring is so late in
coming," said the Selfish Giant, as he sat at the window
and looked out at his cold white garden; "I hope there
will be a change in the weather."

But the Spring never came, nor the Summer. The

Autumn gave golden fruit to every garden, but to the Giant's garden she gave none. "He is too selfish," she said. So it was always Winter there, and the North Wind, and the Hail, and the Frost, and the Snow danced about through the trees.

One morning the Giant was lying awake in bed when he heard some lovely music. It sounded so sweet to his ears that he thought it must be the King's musicians passing by. It was really only a little linnet singing outside his window, but it was so long since he had heard a bird sing in his garden that it seemed to him to be the most beautiful music in the world. Then the Hail stopped dancing over his head, and the North Wind ceased roaring, and a delicious perfume came to him through the open casement. "I believe the Spring has come at last," said the Giant; and he jumped out of bed and looked out.

What did he see?

He saw a most wonderful sight. Through a little hole in the wall the children had crept in, and they were sitting in the branches of the trees. In every tree that he could see

自
私
的
巨
人

there was a little child. And the trees were so glad to have the children back again that they had covered themselves with blossoms, and were waving their arms gently above the children's heads. The birds were flying about and twittering with delight, and the flowers were looking up through the green grass and laughing. It was a lovely scene, only in one corner it was still winter. It was the farthest corner of the garden, and in it was standing a little boy. He was so small that he could not reach up to the branches of the tree, and he was wandering all round it, crying bitterly. The poor tree was still quite covered with frost and snow, and the North Wind was blowing and roaring above it. "Climb up! little boy," said the Tree, and it bent its branches down as low as it could; but the boy was too tiny.

And the Giant's heart melted as he looked out. "How selfish I have been!" he said; "now I know why the Spring would not come here. I will put that poor little boy on the top of the tree, and then I will knock down the wall, and my garden shall be the children's playground for ever and ever." He was really very sorry for what he had done.

So he crept downstairs and opened the front door quite softly, and went out into the garden. But when the children saw him they were so frightened that they all ran away, and the garden became winter again. Only the little boy did not run, for his eyes were so full of tears that he did not see the Giant coming. And the Giant stole up behind him and took him gently in his hand, and put him up into the tree. And the tree broke at once into blossom, and the birds came and sang on it, and the little boy stretched out his two arms and flung them round the Giant's neck, and kissed him. And the other children, when they saw that the Giant was not wicked any longer, came running back, and with them came the Spring. "It is your garden now, little children," said the Giant, and he took a great axe and knocked down the wall. And when the people were going to market at twelve o'clock they found the Giant playing with the children in the most beautiful garden they had ever seen.

All day long they played, and in the evening they

自
私
的
巨
人

came to the Giant to bid him good-bye.

"But where is your little companion?" he said: "the boy I put into the tree."The Giant loved him the best because he had kissed him.

"We don't know," answered the children; "he has gone away."

"You must tell him to be sure and come here tomorrow," said the Giant. But the children said that they did not know where he lived, and had never seen him before; and the Giant felt very sad.

Every afternoon, when school was over, the children came and played with the Giant. But the little boy whom the Giant loved was never seen again. The Giant was very kind to all the children, yet he longed for his first little friend, and often spoke of him. "How I would like to see him!" he used to say.

Years went over, and the Giant grew very old and feeble. He could not play about any more, so he sat in a huge armchair, and watched the children at their games, and admired his garden. "I have many beautiful

夜
莺
与
玫
瑰

304

flowers," he said; "but the children are the most beautiful flowers of all."

One winter morning he looked out of his window as he was dressing. He did not hate the Winter now, for he knew that it was merely the Spring asleep, and that the flowers were resting.

Suddenly he rubbed his eyes in wonder, and looked and looked. It certainly was a marvelous sight. In the farthest corner of the garden was a tree quite covered with lovely white blossoms. Its branches were all golden, and silver fruit hung down from them, and underneath it stood the little boy he had loved.

Downstairs ran the Giant in great joy, and out into the garden. He hastened across the grass, and came near to the child. And when he came quite close his face grew red with anger, and he said, "Who hath dared to wound thee?" For on the palms of the child's hands were the prints of two nails, and the prints of two nails were on the little feet.

"Who hath dared to wound thee?" cried the Giant; "tell

自
私
的
巨
人

me, that I may take my big sword and slay him."

"Nay!" answered the child; "but these are the wounds of Love."

"Who art thou?" said the Giant, and a strange awe fell on him, and he knelt before the little child.

And the child smiled on the Giant, and said to him, "You let me play once in your garden, today you shall come with me to my garden, which is Paradise."

And when the children ran in that afternoon, they found the Giant lying dead under the tree, all covered with white blossoms.

图书在版编目（CIP）数据

夜莺与玫瑰：中英对照彩绘珍藏版：汉英对照／（英）奥斯卡·王尔德（Oscar Wilde）著；林徽因译；张叔筠绘.—北京：化学工业出版社，2016.10（2024.5重印）

书名原文：The Nightingale and the Rose

ISBN 978-7-122-27987-3

Ⅰ.①夜… Ⅱ.①奥…②林…③张… Ⅲ.①通话-作品集-英国-近代-汉、英 Ⅳ.①I561.88

中国版本图书馆CIP数据核字（2016）第210179号

责任编辑：马　骄　梁郁菲　　　　　装帧设计：尹琳琳

责任校对：王素芹

出版发行：化学工业出版社（北京市东城区青年湖南街 13 号　邮政编码 100011）

印　　装：北京建宏印刷有限公司

880mm×1230mm　1/32　印张10　字数156千字　2024 年 5 月北京第 1 版第 2 次印刷

购书咨询：010-64518888　　　　　售后服务：010-64518899

网　　址：http://www.cip.com.cn

凡购买本书，如有缺损质量问题，本社销售中心负责调换。

定　　价：58.00 元　　　　　　　　　　　版权所有　违者必究